Cambridge Elements

Elements in the Psychology of Religion
edited by
Jonathan Lewis-Jong
St Mary's University Twickenham and University of Oxford

THE PSYCHOLOGY OF MYSTICISM

Zhuo Job Chen
University of North Carolina at Charlotte

Shaftesbury Road, Cambridge CB2 8EA, United Kingdom

One Liberty Plaza, 20th Floor, New York, NY 10006, USA

477 Williamstown Road, Port Melbourne, VIC 3207, Australia

314–321, 3rd Floor, Plot 3, Splendor Forum, Jasola District Centre, New Delhi – 110025, India

103 Penang Road, #05–06/07, Visioncrest Commercial, Singapore 238467

Cambridge University Press is part of Cambridge University Press & Assessment, a department of the University of Cambridge.

We share the University's mission to contribute to society through the pursuit of education, learning and research at the highest international levels of excellence.

www.cambridge.org
Information on this title: www.cambridge.org/9781009663311

DOI: 10.1017/9781009420860

© Zhuo Job Chen 2026

This publication is in copyright. Subject to statutory exception and to the provisions of relevant collective licensing agreements, no reproduction of any part may take place without the written permission of Cambridge University Press & Assessment.

When citing this work, please include a reference to the DOI 10.1017/9781009420860

First published 2026

A catalogue record for this publication is available from the British Library

ISBN 978-1-009-66331-1 Hardback
ISBN 978-1-009-42087-7 Paperback
ISSN 2753-6866 (online)
ISSN 2753-6858 (print)

Cambridge University Press & Assessment has no responsibility for the persistence or accuracy of URLs for external or third-party internet websites referred to in this publication and does not guarantee that any content on such websites is, or will remain, accurate or appropriate.

For EU product safety concerns, contact us at Calle de José Abascal, 56, 1°, 28003 Madrid, Spain, or email eugpsr@cambridge.org

The Psychology of Mysticism

Elements in the Psychology of Religion

DOI: 10.1017/9781009420860
First published online: January 2026

Zhuo Job Chen
University of North Carolina at Charlotte
Author for correspondence: Zhuo Job Chen, job.chen@charlotte.edu

Abstract: Mysticism refers to extraordinary experiences that transcend perceived reality and transform the individual. Section 1 introduces key features such as noetic and ineffable qualities, alongside psychological typologies and a fourfold Layered Hierachy Model of mysticism. Section 2 explores monistic mysticism, where self and ultimate reality merge in oneness and ego dissolution, illustrated through perennial philosophy and its critiques. Section 3 examines nondualistic mysticism, in which the self remains distinct yet is absorbed into a transcendent order, exemplified in world religions where the ego yields to the divine. Section 4 discusses dualistic mysticism, where the self encounters a separate nonhuman reality, often expressed through shamanism, spiritist visions, and psychedelic states. Section 5 presents pluralistic mysticism, emphasizing multiple dimensions of self and reality, integrating embodied and spiritual aspects, and drawing on nonphysicalism and parapsychology. Section 6 synthesizes these perspectives, stressing that transcendent realities require self-transformation and that mystical insights can inform daily life across culture.

Keywords: mysticism, psychedelics, consciousness, spirituality, religion

© Zhuo Job Chen 2026

ISBNs: 9781009663311 (HB), 9781009420877 (PB), 9781009420860 (OC)
ISSNs: 2753-6866 (online), 2753-6858 (print)

Contents

1. Definition and Model of Mysticism — 1
2. Monistic Mysticism — 10
3. Nondualistic Mysticism — 18
4. Dualistic Mysticism — 30
5. Pluralistic Mysticism — 41
6. Philosophical Reflections — 51

References — 61

1 Definition and Model of Mysticism

The etymology of the English term "mystic" traces back to the ancient Greek Eleusinian rites, where initiates were required to remain silent (*muein*) about the details of the ceremony, giving rise to the Greek term *mustikos* (i.e., initiates). It denotes an encounter that transcends worldly description and is withheld from non-initiates. Similar meanings are found, for example, in Chinese, *shen mi*, "divine secrets." Therefore, mysticism denotes an experience that extends beyond perceived reality and its linguistic representation.

This return to the linguistic root aligns with William James's (1902) classical definition, which identifies two essential characteristics of mysticism: the noetic and the ineffable. The noetic aspect refers to insights apprehended through direct intuitive knowledge, pointing to a deeper understanding of reality, while the ineffable pertains to experiences that transcend the limits of language. Together, these elements define mysticism as an encounter that pushes the boundaries of perceived reality and transforms the perceiver, culminating in an indescribable state of revelation. This extends the definition and scope of mysticism, encompassing all extraordinary experiences that meet these two criteria – *a transcendence of perceived reality* and *a transformation of the individual*.

Mysticism has been defined and understood in various ways, often emphasizing an altered state of consciousness distinct from the daily mundane one (Tart, 1972). The human longing for something beyond perceived reality frequently initiates the mystical journey (Weiner, 1969). As such, mysticism encompasses concepts that transcend the ordinary, often described using terms such as exceptional, extraordinary, nonordinary, ecstatic, paranormal, supernormal, and altered. For instance, Murphy (1992) characterizes mystical experiences as altered states that reveal deeper truths, where the "supernormal" refers to unconscious abilities brought under conscious control. Similarly, Merkur (2010) frames mysticism as the practice of religious ecstatic states of consciousness, accompanied by corresponding ideologies. Given our expanded definition, this Element adopts an inclusive approach, using the term mysticism to encompass a wide range of experiences otherwise labeled differently, as long as they align with the core criteria outlined in our framework.

This Element examines the psychology of mysticism while integrating insights from religious, anthropological, and philosophical perspectives. Unlike philosophical approaches that consider the ontological status of mystical experiences, religious studies that focus on historical texts, or anthropological analyses that compare mystical practices across societies, the psychological perspective, with its emphasis on consciousness, prioritizes individual experiences. It values self-reported observations, employs empirical methodologies, and analyzes descriptive accounts of mystical states. From this viewpoint, while the objects of mysticism may be unverifiable or metaphysically elusive, the psychological impact of the experience itself remains valid and significant (Staal, 1975). In exploring mysticism, the focus shifts from what elicits the experience to the psychological state of the individual undergoing it.

The following sections expand on the noetic and ineffable qualities that define mysticism, clarify its definition, present representative typologies and measurements in psychological research, and finally, introduce the layered hierarchy model that will be explored in depth throughout this Element.

1.1 Noetic and Ineffable

Noetic knowledge refers to insight gained directly – often through bodily experience, intuitions, visions, and revelations that reach beyond sensory processing or rational thought. These modes of knowing illustrate how mystical insight transcends the limits of ordinary perception and reasoning. They open onto a deeper grasp of reality, one that is difficult to articulate yet profoundly meaningful to those who encounter it. As Blavatsky (1895) observed, the essence of truth cannot be fully conveyed in words or writing but must be discovered within one's own inner experience.

Mystical knowledge often takes the form of a direct perception of reality. In this sense, mysticism resembles science in its systematic inquiry into the nature of the world – yet whereas science focuses on external phenomena, mystics seek understanding through inner experience (Radin, 1997). Mysticism thus culminates in a form of knowing detached from sensory or mental imagery (Smart, 1965). Huxley (1954) draws a sharp contrast between mystical insight and rational or systematic reasoning, defining mysticism as a direct apprehension of reality that surpasses discursive thought while still being wholly and immediately grasped.

A key element in this process is intuition, which serves as a bridge between external symbols and inner understanding. Rooted in Aristotle's notion of *nous*, often translated as intuitive reason, intuition involves the direct apprehension of primary, self-evident principles (Bolton, 2014). For Coomaraswamy (1977), intuition allows us to grasp the truths behind symbols, which themselves only point toward deeper meanings. Thus, symbols derive significance not from their own content but from the transcendent realities they reveal.

Mystical traditions also speak of "knowledge by identity," in which one knows by becoming one with what is known (Kelly et al., 2015). Unlike ordinary knowledge, which presupposes a gap between subject and object, this mode of knowing fuses the two. The faculty that mediates such knowledge is gnosis, a direct and immediate form of understanding. Meister Eckhart described this as a "pure intellect" uniting with its object without separation. In this framework, experiencing something confers its reality, a point developed by Shanon (2002) under the notion of the "conferral of reality." Similarly, Merleau-Ponty (1962) emphasized that perception does more than register details about objects; it also affirms their existence. To experience something is thus already to believe in its reality. Huxley (1954) extended this insight by suggesting that mystical awareness can encompass all that happens everywhere in the universe. He further proposed that attaining such superconscious states requires passing through the subconscious, one pathway being the chemistry of the individual cell – an anticipation of what might be called embodied spirituality, or knowing through becoming.

Mystical experiences are often described as ineffable because they involve a profound transformation of the self, making them resistant to verbal expression. In such states, ordinary cognitive processes are suspended, leaving no framework for articulating the experience. This raises a central question: if such experiences are ineffable, how can they yield knowledge? A common explanation is that while discursive reasoning falls silent during the experience itself, it resumes afterward, enabling interpretation and communication of the insights received.

Another crucial question follows: Is there still a perceiver once everything disappears from consciousness? The answer given by most accounts is yes. With the dissolution of the governing ego, a different form of self-awareness emerges. This self is not the familiar "I" of ordinary reasoning but a deeper awareness that observes and exists independently of egoic constructs. Obeyesekere (2012) describes this agency as grounded not in the "I" but in what Nietzsche (1909) termed the "It," as in his famous remark: "A thought comes when it wishes, and not when 'I' wish" (p. 24). Nietzsche's critique unsettles the Cartesian dictum "I think, therefore I am," suggesting instead that thought arises spontaneously, apart from the ego's control. Freud's *The Ego and the Id* might be more precisely translated as *The I and the It*, reflecting the distinction between the conscious self and a deeper, impersonal agency.

Although mysticism resists articulation, it is expected to enlighten and transform the way one relates to reality. In classical Jewish thought, for example, clarity of perception – not a "cloud of unknowing" – is taken as the mark of true mystical experience (Weiner, 1969). A claim to profound truth must engage both feeling and reason. This is why Moses, to whom the concrete laws and historical narratives of the Tanakh are attributed, is regarded as the Jewish mystic *par excellence*. Unlike other prophets who apprehended truth as if through a dim mirror, Moses is said to have seen it as though through a clear glass. The communicability and clarity of his vision testify to a face-to-face encounter with divine reality.

Because mysticism carries both noetic depth and ineffability, it has sometimes fostered elitism and rigidity in asserting exclusive truth. Such tensions have accompanied mysticism across the centuries and continue in the present. This Element, however, argues from a pluralistic standpoint that mysticism should cultivate inclusivity and openness, always widening its horizon of possibilities. Each mystical encounter should be treated not as a final revelation but as a gateway to further exploration, reminding us that there is always more to uncover and understand.

With these extended explanations in mind, three conceptual pairs emerge in defining mysticism as *transcendence of perceived reality and transformation of the individual*: self and reality, transcendence and transformation, and the noetic and the ineffable. Their interrelations can be described as follows. Prior to a mystical encounter, the individual self perceives and engages with reality in an ordinary way. Mysticism transcends this perception, opening onto a noetic grasp – an intuitive knowledge of a deeper dimension. Simultaneously, it transforms the individual so that their mode of interaction with reality is no longer the same. Ineffability, in this context, does not merely indicate what cannot be described because language and cognition fall short; it also renders ordinary modes of action inadequate, since action itself is a form of articulation. In this sense, mysticism moderates and modifies the interaction between self and reality, reshaping both perception and participation. Figure 1 provides a schematic view of our definition of mysticism.

1.2 Types and Measures

There are numerous ways to classify mysticism, with psychological assessments of such experiences relying primarily on self-reports (Jones & Gellman, 2022). Classical classifications, echoing Greek irrationalism (Dodds, 1964), often propose broad categories based on general psychological features. Naranjo (1976) identifies three types of meditative states: the negative way, the middle way, and the expressive way. The negative way emphasizes elimination, detachment, and emptiness, pursuing a path of inner emptiness. This idea is akin to the *via negativa*, an iconoclastic turn in mysticism in which forms attributed to the divine are regarded as limiting rather than revealing, and the mystical path is understood as the removal of such obscurations. From this perspective arises the concept of ineffability. The middle way involves concentration, absorption, and union, characterized as outer-directed and aligned with

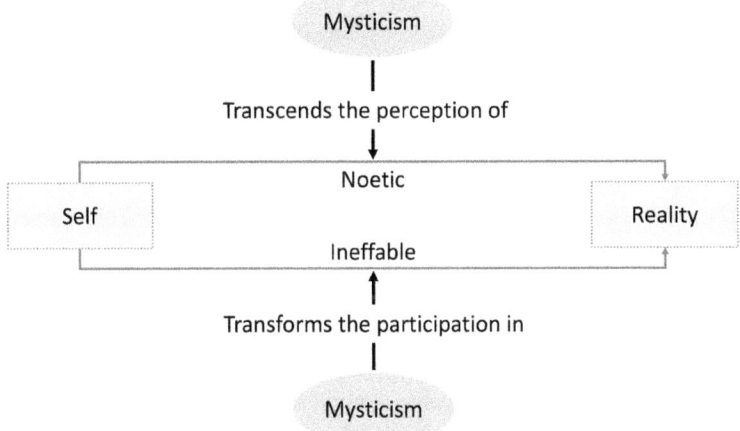

Figure 1 Theoretical model of defining mysticism as transcending the perceived reality and transforming the individual.

an Apollonian orientation. The expressive way, by contrast, highlights freedom, transparency, and surrender, embodying an inner-directed, Dionysian orientation. Another influential scheme distinguishes between functional and nonfunctional mysticism (Paper, 2004). Functional ecstasies include visions, problem-solving dreams, shamanism, mediumship, and prophecy – experiences with practical implications. Nonfunctional ecstasies, in contrast, encompass unitive states, pure consciousness, and encounters with nonself, with the emphasis placed on transcending utility.

A common approach to understanding extraordinary experiences is to enumerate known examples, and measurement instruments have often adopted this strategy, asking respondents to identify or classify their own experiences. White (1997), for example, cataloged approximately 100 exceptional human experiences, organizing them into five categories: psychic, encounter, death-related, unitive, and exceptional but normal (e.g., dreams). More recent studies propose empirically derived categories such as numinous, revelatory, synchronistic, aesthetic, paranormal, and mystical experiences (Yaden & Newberg, 2022). Standard textbooks in the psychology of religion likewise include discussions of paranormal experiences that overlap with religious and spiritual phenomena (e.g., Hood et al., 2018). Some scales explicitly target paranormal-like experiences, such as nonlocal consciousness, extraterrestrial contact, precognition, survival of consciousness, communication with the dead, clairvoyance, psychokinesis, telepathy, and automatism. Examples include the Noetic Experience and Belief Scale (Wahbeh et al., 2020) and an earlier, more comprehensive Anomalous

Experiences Inventory (Gallagher, 1994). At the other end of the spectrum are scales that measure more ordinary experiences of transcendence in daily life, such as awe, gratitude, mercy, connection with the transcendent, and compassionate love, as captured in the Daily Spiritual Experience Scale (Underwood, 2011).

The dominant psychological model of mysticism, focused on unitive experience, is grounded in the classification of core features first outlined by James (1902) and Otto (1932), and later expanded by Stace (1960). This framework identifies two experiential factors: the introvertive factor, marked by the dissolution of self and spatiotemporal transcendence; and the extrovertive factor, entailing unity with the world and recognition of the subjectivity within all things. A third interpretive factor captures the appraisal of experience in terms of positive affect, sacredness, noetic quality, and ineffability. Importantly, not all mystical experiences are positive: Otto (1917), for instance, explicitly described the frightening and awe-inspiring aspect of the divine in his concept of the *mysterium tremendum*. Nevertheless, this three-factor model was operationalized in the Mysticism Scale (Hood, 1975), which has been validated cross-culturally, with a brief eight-item version also available (Streib & Chen, 2021). Related measures assessing mystical states occasioned by psychedelics have likewise been developed, beginning with Pahnke's (1969) work and culminating in the Mystical Experience Questionnaire (MEQ; Barrett et al., 2015), emphasizing mystical unity, positive mood, transcendence of time and space, and ineffability.

One major critique of preceding measures is that they conflate appraisal, affect, and phenomenology, as seen in the MEQ's emphasis on positive states, leaving little room for negatively valenced mystical experiences. Challenging this narrow focus on alterations in selfhood, Taves and Barlev (2023) advanced a feature-based approach that distinguishes phenomenological features of experiences from their appraisals in interview protocols. The Inventory of Nonordinary Experiences (Taves et al., 2023) reflects this updated understanding by incorporating a broader range of lesser-studied phenomena, including experiences of Kundalini energy, possession states, and unitive mysticism.

Qualitative studies are particularly useful in capturing nuances that structured self-report questionnaires may overlook. One line of research has adapted Hood's scale into qualitative investigations of various traditions, including Buddhists (Chen et al., 2011a), Daoists (Chen et al., 2023; Chen & Guo, 2025), North American shamans (Chen, 2023), and soul-mate relationships (Chen & Patel, 2021). Another approach has examined the varieties of contemplative experience among American Buddhists (Lindahl et al., 2017), employing open-ended questions alongside detailed coding manuals that categorize cognitive, affective, somatic, and self-related changes.

A comprehensive anthropological study conducted in the US, Ghana, China, and Vanuatu examined the experience of sensing the presence of gods, resulting in the development of the Spiritual Events Scale and the concept of Porosity – the idea that spirits can influence human thoughts and feelings, sometimes even causing harm (Luhrmann et al., 2021). The Spiritual Events Interview further explored how individuals perceive divine presence through auditory experiences, dreams, visual phenomena, bodily sensations, and encounters with supernatural beings, leading to the development of quantitative scales.

Certain personality and aptitudes are inducive to mysticism. Thalbourne and Delin (1994) coined the term "transliminal" to describe a common underlying factor characterized by an involuntary susceptibility to inwardly generated psychological phenomena of an ideational and affective kind. The resulting Transliminality Scale (Chen & Ghorbani, 2024; Houran et al., 2003) measures an aptitude for heightened sensory perception and a tendency for absorption – a disposition for experiencing episodes of total attention that fully engage one's representational resources (Tellegen & Atkinson, 1974).

Mystical states can arise either spontaneously or under a variety of religious and spiritual contexts that offer techniques designed to induce mysticism. Shamanism, for instance, has developed systematic methods for inducing altered states of consciousness, such as through visualization or rhythmic drumming (Harner, 1980). In laboratory-controlled settings, numerous ways have been developed to elicit different mystical states (for a review, see Ludwig, 1966). These techniques are often ironically contrasting, including reduction of stimuli (e.g., isolation tanks; Hood & Morris, 1981) and enhancement of external stimuli (e.g., stress; Hood, 1977), as well as techniques that increase both alertness and relaxation (e.g., concentrative meditation; Deikman, 1966).

With the recent exploration of psychedelic drugs for psychiatric treatment, psychedelics can reliably trigger unitive mystical experiences (Merkur, 1998), both with psilocybin (Griffiths et al., 2006) and lysergic acid diethylamide (LSD; Carhart-Harris, 2016). The variety of conditions that occasion mystical experience highlights the complexity of this issue. A single stimulus can produce various states of consciousness, while different stimuli can also result in the same type of conscious state. Physiological states are neither necessary nor sufficient for the experience to occur.

1.3 Layered Hierarchy Model

This brief review shows that mysticism is an encompassing category that incorporates a wide range of extraordinary human experiences. The central issue lies in definitions, which shape how one conceptualizes and maps different forms of

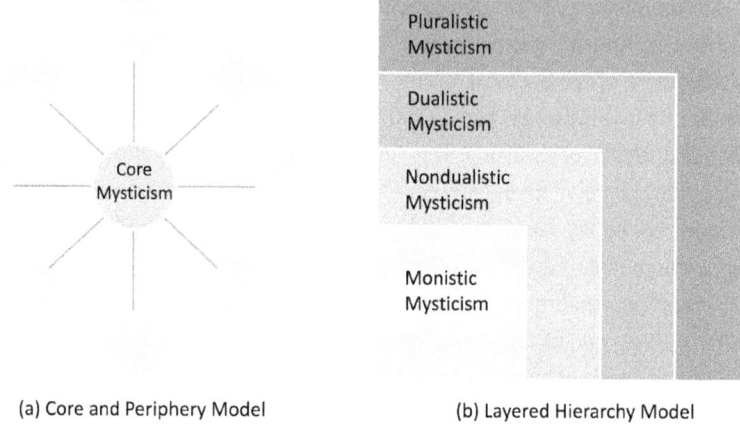

Figure 2 Two different conceptual models of mysticism.

mysticism. One influential perspective is the core–periphery model, depicted in Figure 2a, which locates a mystical core, such as union with the Absolute, as the ultimate truth of reality, set apart from peripheral experiences that attach this core to particular deities or traditions. This, however, is not the view we adopt. Instead, we propose a layered hierarchy model of mysticism, depicted in Figure 2b, and illustrate its layers – monistic, nondualistic, dualistic, and pluralistic – each representing a distinct configuration of perceived reality, the individual self, and the patterns of interaction between self and reality. While neither exhaustive nor definitive, the aim of this model is to chart the complex terrain of extraordinary experiences and to offer one way of understanding the variety of human experiences and the possible meanings behind them.

The layered hierarchy model diverges from the core-periphery model in several fundamental ways. Rather than serving as a mere classification system for extraordinary human experiences, it rejects the notion that different mystical states exist as discrete, non-overlapping categories. It neither implies a hierarchical ranking of importance or progression nor suggests that one form of mysticism is more "real" than another. Instead, this framework provides a lens through which extraordinary experiences are understood as transcending human perceptions of reality by integrating both physical (body) and nonphysical (consciousness) aspects.

In the layered hierarchy model, monistic mysticism emphasizes the experience of oneness, where all reality is perceived as a unified whole, and the self dissolves entirely into infinite emptiness, rendering the body formless and irrelevant. This perspective is prevalent in perennialism and the concept of a unitive common core. Nondualistic mysticism introduces a higher reality beyond the mundane world, where the self partially submits to an idealized divine presence, often regarding the body as an obstacle to the soul's liberation. Such experiences are commonly embedded within mystical traditions across various religions. Dualistic mysticism, by contrast, maintains a clear distinction between human and nonhuman realms, often involving interactions with spiritual beings or transcendent forces. Within this framework, the self remains distinct yet engages with the spirit world, with the body serving as a vessel for divine teachings, as seen in spiritism or certain psychedelic states. Pluralistic mysticism, meanwhile, embraces the coexistence of multiple realities, with the self manifesting in diverse forms and the body regarded as integral to realizing spiritual potential. This perspective is frequently expressed in nonphysicalism and parapsychological perspectives. Table 1 provides a summary of these four layers, aligning with an expanded definition of mysticism – one that encompasses both the transcendence of perceived reality and the transformation of the perceiver.

Table 1 Summary of the four layers of mysticism.

Layers of mysticism	Transcends the self's perception of reality	Transforms the self and its participation in reality	Some examples
Monistic mysticism	Awareness of reality is experience itself	No self: Dissolution of ego and unification with all existence	Perennialism, unitive experience
Nondualistic mysticism	A higher and ideal reality beyond the perceived one	One: Recognition of an idealized divine and subjugation of the self to it	Numinous experience, religions
Dualistic mysticism	Spiritual realms in contrast to the human realm	Two: Separation and interaction of the individual self and spiritual beings	Psychedelic experience, spiritism
Pluralistic mysticism	Numerous realities, multiverses coexist	Myriad: Coexistence of multiplicity of the self and realities	Nonphysicalism, parapsychology

In our model, both "layer" and "hierarchy" carry distinct meanings. The hierarchical arrangement of these layers reflects multiple dimensions. First, it represents varying levels of transcendence in perceived reality, ranging from the ultimate unity of all things to the multiplicity of physical and non-physical worlds. Second, it addresses the transformation of selfhood, spanning from complete dissolution to a well-defined sense of agency, with multiple possible agents emerging within the experience. Third, it concerns the degree to which the body is involved, ranging from total irrelevance to being indispensable for the experience. The fourth dimension pertains to cultural influences – monistic experiences, being devoid of specific content, are least shaped by cultural and cognitive framing, whereas the outer layers are more susceptible to situational and interpretive factors. The layered structure also highlights the overlap between different types of mysticism: nondualistic mysticism encompasses elements of monistic mysticism, dualistic mysticism incorporates aspects of both nondualistic and monistic mysticism, and pluralistic mysticism integrates aspects of all three. This perspective preserves the possibility that a common unitive core may exist at every experiential layer.

2 Monistic Mysticism

The first layer, monistic mysticism, posits a single ultimate reality experienced as a profound awareness of unity with the cosmic consciousness. In this state, the distinction between perceiver and experience vanishes; awareness and experience merge into one. This form of mysticism transcends perceived reality by revealing the fundamental oneness of all existence and transforms the individual through the dissolution of selfhood. This section will first describe the philosophical tradition of perennialism, which emphasizes a universal principle underlying all traditions. Next, it will examine unitive mysticism and the common core thesis in psychology, which seeks to identify shared experiential elements across traditions. Following this, social constructionist critiques of the common core thesis and essentialism will be presented and addressed. Finally, a modified common core thesis will be introduced, balancing the universality of human psychological processes with cultural specificity.

2.1 Perennial Philosophy

This position finds its strongest advocate in what is known as the perennial philosophy, eloquently articulated by Aldous Huxley (1945) as "the metaphysic that recognizes a divine Reality substantial to the world of things and lives and minds; the psychology that finds in the soul something similar to, or even identical with, divine Reality; the ethic that places man's final end in the knowledge of the immanent and transcendent Ground of all being – the thing is immemorial and universal" (p. 4). The origins of the perennial philosophy may be traced to the sixteenth century, when it emerged as a Renaissance vision of a primordial religion underlying all religions, subsequently expressed in diverse forms (Kripal, 2008). This constitutes the narrow sense of perennialism as the unification of beliefs and traditions.

The core assertion of perennialism is that truth is one, everywhere, and always the same. This universal truth underlies all religious and spiritual traditions, cutting across cultural boundaries. Ultimate reality is regarded as accessible to human consciousness through direct spiritual experience. In poetic terms, much like a perennial flower that blossoms year after year, truth is repeatedly unveiled to humanity. Without insisting upon surface-level similarities among traditions, perennialists argue that authentic revelations and practices have been providentially given to specific peoples, each sufficient for guiding humanity toward its ultimate end (Cutsinger, 1997).

Perennialism boasts a long and vibrant intellectual history, often celebrated as an unbroken continuity of thought. It includes authors who identify sublime principles – some transcendent source of all realities – as perennial (Faivre, 1994). Among them are ancient Greek philosophers such as Pythagoras and Plato; Hellenistic and early Christian thinkers like Ammonius Saccas and Origen; Gnostic and Neoplatonic figures such as Plotinus and Iamblichus; early Christian theologians like Dionysius the Areopagite and Augustine of Hippo; Renaissance thinkers such as Marsilio Ficino and Nicholas of Cusa; and Hermeticists like Paracelsus and Jacob Boehme. Contributions also come from medieval Islamic philosophers, Christian mystics, and Jewish Kabbalists, who will be discussed in Section 3 on nondualistic mysticism, while modern esotericists such as Blavatsky and the Theosophical Society will be considered in Section 4 on dualistic mysticism.

Several key twentieth-century figures are recognized as pioneers of the so-called traditionalist school, which revived and promoted perennial philosophy. Ananda Coomaraswamy (1943), noted for his exploration of traditional metaphysics and symbolism in Eastern religions, sought to uncover a unifying core among seemingly disparate traditions. René Guénon (1945), a French metaphysician, advocated a return to esoteric wisdom grounded in universal principles underlying all manifestation. His disciple Fritjof Schuon (1953) further developed the notion of a transcendent unity of religions. A summary of perennialist writings, including extensive quotations from diverse religious and esoteric traditions, can be found in Perry (1981).

Yet the absolute and often dogmatic claims of perennial philosophy invite several criticisms. The foremost critique is the lack of evidence supporting the doctrine of the unity of all religions (Staal, 1975). This doctrine appears to be a construct of a group of spiritual illuminati promoting a new religious movement aimed at unifying, or perhaps challenging, existing religions. A more pluralistic and context-sensitive approach to esotericism is therefore advocated, one grounded in historical, textual, and descriptive analysis rather than subsuming diverse traditions under a universal category (Huss, 2020).

Another line of critique is that perennialism tends to mirror truths propagated by Western imperialism. For example, rather than urging reverence for the ongoing cycles of human and natural life or honoring the spirits of the land without ownership, perennialist truths often resemble a deistic framework familiar to Western civilizations. In other words, representations of the East are filtered through a lens of power serving imperial interests (Said, 1978). Systematic criticism of this perspective has emphasized that not all societies follow Europe's developmental trajectory, and Europe is not essential for understanding non-Western experiences (Chakrabarty, 2020).

Finally, a central tenet of perennial philosophy – that Truth and the Way precede life – requires acceptance of prescribed wisdom as the condition for a meaningful existence. Yet perennialism is not a pragmatic framework; mere assent to the doctrine of universality does little to improve daily life. As Nasr (1981) argues, one cannot have immanence without transcendence: the transformative encounter with the divine is essential to perceiving the cosmos as theophany. Without such lived experience, the universal spiritual vision of perennial philosophy remains abstract and disconnected from practical human concerns.

2.2 Common Unitive Core

The pursuit of universal truth within perennial philosophy provides a foundation for the psychological study of unitive experiences. The claim that a common wisdom underlies diverse spiritual traditions suggests a phenomenological unity between perceiver and perceived reality. While unity is singular in essence, it manifests in distinct forms. One such form is extrovertive unity, in which the self merges with all things, perceiving reality in its totality without imposed categorization – a state encapsulated in Bucke's (1923) notion of cosmic consciousness. This entails an awareness of the cosmos as intrinsically alive and ordered, accompanied by a sense of eternal existence, as undying consciousness is experienced as already present. Another form is introvertive unity, which divides into two states: one with awareness and one without. In the awareness state, ego is not lost; the experiencer observes the experience and can recall it later, even when infused with a profound sense of nonself. Forman (1999) describes this as the pure consciousness state, an unchanging interior silence that coexists with intentional experience. By contrast, the no-awareness state occurs when, at the height of the experience, the experiencer is entirely unaware of its occurrence. Jones (1986) calls this depth mysticism, in which there is no direct apprehension of unity but rather an awareness that itself constitutes the experience. This form of unity closely parallels nondualist Vedanta, particularly the *turiya* state described in the Mandukya Upanishad (2–7), which transcends waking, dreaming, and deep sleep. *Turiya* is characterized as neither inward nor outward, ineffable, beyond duality, and defined by unwavering conviction in the oneness of self, causing the phenomenal world to dissolve.

These different types of unity are experiences rather than beliefs, untethered from specific content. This feature is crucial: when a person reports an experience of oneness – whether perceiving all things as part of the same whole or merging with all things – the object of unity remains unspecified, leaving interpretation open to cultural variation. A Neoplatonist may describe it as union with "the One"; an Eckhartian Christian may identify it with the Godhead; a Sufi may interpret it as *Tawhid*; and a Daoist may understand it as the Way. Yet despite these doctrinal differences, the pure experience of oneness recurs across mystical writings. This striking consistency led William James (1902), adopting radical empiricism, to conclude: "In Hinduism, in Neo-Platonism, in Sufism, in Christian Mysticism, in Whitmanism, we find the same recurring note" (p. 332).

Building on this observation, the common core thesis asserts that a universal experiential core exists across cultures and can be empirically identified (Hood, 2006). Hood's 32-item Mysticism Scale (1975) operationalizes this core through three factors: an introvertive factor of ego loss and spatiotemporal transcendence; an extrovertive factor of unitive vision and the inner subjectivity of all beings; and an interpretive factor encompassing sacredness, bliss, noetic quality, and ineffability. In psychological studies, respondents rate the extent to which they have experienced these phenomena (e.g., for ego loss: "everything has disappeared from mind until you are conscious only of a void"). Factor analysis, which groups responses based on patterns of association, has shown that this three-factor structure holds across diverse religious and cultural contexts, including American Christians (Williamson et al., 2019), Chinese Buddhist monastics (Chen et al., 2011a), Chinese Christians and religious nones (Chen et al., 2012), Iranian Muslims (Chen et al., 2013), and Tibetan Buddhists (Chen et al., 2011b). While studies using the Mysticism Scale evaluate whether the structural arrangement of mystical facets aligns with empirical data – without directly probing the specific content of experiences or the comparability of interpretations across traditions – the scale's successful cross-cultural application suggests that unitive experience, though abstract and devoid of specific content, can nonetheless be meaningfully recognized across diverse cultural and linguistic contexts.

2.3 Criticism and Response

The common core thesis and monistic mysticism have been subject to sustained critique from social constructionism, which holds that reality emerges through cultural and linguistic processes and that observation is never entirely free of context. From this perspective, essentialist claims about mystical experience are undermined: the perception of unity does not correspond to an independent reality, and mysticism should not be treated as a discrete domain. Sharf (1998) and contributors to Katz's edited volumes (1978, 1992) reject the notion that mystical experiences are private, inner events existing apart from cultural frameworks. For Sharf, while experiences do occur, the very category of "experience" functions less as an objective reality than as an academic construct that legitimizes particular interests. In short, mysticism, according to constructionists, derives meaning from public discourse and shared cultural traditions rather than from experience itself.

On a more moderate level, mystical experiences are taken to be culturally conditioned narratives, rituals, and expressions rather than unmediated inner events. Thus, monistic mysticism cannot be detached from the traditions in which it is embedded (Katz, 1978). The congruence of mystical experiences across traditions is rendered impossible by historical and cultural particularization (Proudfoot, 1985). Proudfoot further argues that beliefs and attitudes shape experience, rather than result from it, determining in advance what kinds of experiences are even possible. From this vantage point, mysticism differs fundamentally across traditions. Katz's subsequent edited volumes situate mystical writings within their respective religious milieus (Katz, 1983), align them with sacred scriptures (Katz, 2000), and anthologize texts devoted to mystical doctrines and practices (Katz, 2013). Covering Judaism, Christianity, Sufism, Hinduism, Buddhism, Confucianism, Daoism, and Native American spirituality, this body of scholarship underscores both the diversity of mystical content and the varied modes of its cultural expression.

Culture not only shapes experience but also governs how it is reported (Bharati, 1961). Mystical reports are never pure transcripts of experience; even Stace (1960) acknowledged that describing an experience inevitably entails interpretation. To address this, characteristics such as bliss, sacredness, noetic quality, and ineffability have been identified as complements to experience – aligned with it but conceptually distinct. Since mystical accounts reflect both felt states and cognitive appraisals, attempts to draw a strict boundary between description and interpretation must account for this overlap.

Methodologically, psychological scales have been criticized for constraining how mystical experience is reported. Predefined factorial structures, rigid question formats, and limited interpretive freedom risk overlooking dimensions of experience not anticipated by the instruments (Belzen, 2009). While self-report remains the dominant method, its validity is uncertain, since it is often unclear whether respondents describe heightened emotion or a mystical state (Greeley, 1975). These philosophical and methodological challenges continue to cast doubt on a monistic common core, even as empirical assessments have identified it across cultures.

Yet the claim that mysticism is nothing more than a cultural construct neglects neurological evidence. Monistic mysticism has been linked to decreased activity in the posterior parietal cortex, which governs spatial awareness and self-other differentiation (Newberg, 2018). This reduction correlates with reported unity and transcendence. Likewise, disrupted connectivity within the default mode network (DMN) – including the medial prefrontal cortex, posterior cingulate cortex, posterior parietal cortex, and temporal regions – has been associated with reported experience of ego dissolution (Siegel et al., 2024). Research on psilocybin and LSD similarly shows significant decreases in activity and connectivity in connector hubs of the brain, facilitating unconstrained cognition (Carhart-Harris et al., 2012, 2016). These decouplings strongly correlate with reports of ego dissolution and altered meaning, highlighting the role of neural circuitry in sustaining selfhood. Long-term contemplative practice also leaves structural traces, such as increased gray matter density in regions tied to emotional regulation and cognitive control (Goleman & Davidson, 2018). Still, as Sarter et al. (1996) caution, neural activity does not correspond one-to-one with experience; brain activity alone cannot explain experience.

While culture shapes mystical expression, one could argue the reverse: that universal principles precede cultural variation. Guinn (1997) contends that sacred principles determine culture rather than merely arise from it. As these principles move from the essential to the substantial – from the principial to the cultural – variations of expression emerge, giving rise to the diversity of traditions. At this level, only motifs or essential principles remain universally recognizable (Campbell, 1949). Moreover, cultural context does not entirely determine the content of mysticism. Many experiences incorporate elements unfamiliar to the individual's religious background, challenging the view that they are wholly constructed (Almond, 1982).

An experience detached from its cultural context may lose some of its interpretive depth, yet this does not invalidate the experience itself. Mystical experiences are authentic psychological phenomena that have been systematically studied in real-time using methods such as autogenic training (Albrecht, 2019). Another critique maintains that if language shapes experience, then ineffable states cannot be genuine experiences. Paper (2004) responds: "While it may be logically impossible for me to have had an ineffable experience – ineffable even to myself – for me it remains a fact that I did indeed have it. Thus, I must either give up on myself or formal logic; my own personal choice I trust is obvious" (p. 55).

Individual construction undeniably plays a role, but at a more fundamental level than social constructivist critiques allow. Belief sets the boundaries of what realities one can access. As the aphorism goes: "For those who believe in God, no explanation is necessary. For those who do not believe in God, no explanation is possible." This ontological divide is exemplified by those who reject dominant normative frameworks in favor of alternative realities, as seen among perennialist commitments. Jung (1953) directly addresses this ontological divide within religious experience, though it could equally apply to mysticism in general: "Religious experience is absolute; it cannot be disputed. You can only say that you have never had such an experience, whereupon your opponent will reply: 'Sorry, I have.' And there your discussion will come to an end" (p. 167). Believers, then, do not speak merely of what they believe, but of what they know to be true – both of reality and of themselves (Jones, 1986).

2.4 Modified Common Core Thesis

These considerations led to a modified common core thesis – one that acknowledges cultural differences while still assessing universality (Chen, 2025). First, the empirically identifiable cluster of mystical experiences does not entail a shared set of higher-order beliefs or practices, as posited by perennial philosophy, nor does it authorize the supremacy of one belief system over another. Moreover, these mystical characteristics do not exhaustively encapsulate private experience, since borderline cases exist where episodes only partially conform to the core features. The common core thesis thus maintains that a unity at the phenomenal level underlies the diversity of religious dogmas and concepts, which emerge as secondary constructs.

Second, reconciliation between the common core thesis and social constructivism may be found in the view that individual beliefs enrich rather than replace mystical experience (Smart, 1965). From this perspective, interpretive systems reshape experiences into culturally intelligible forms. A mediating position holds that mystical experience involves a fundamental transformation of consciousness that transcends doctrinal distinctions, yet its expression remains deeply embedded within particular traditions (Studstill, 2005). Parsons (2018) further argues that mysticism is best studied not in sweeping generalizations but case by case. Precisely because a transcendental core exists, variation in expression acquires comparative significance, reinforcing the claim that "humans are vastly different, with just enough commonalities to enable discourse and empathy" (Parsons, 2018, p. 146). At its most abstract and contentless level, monistic mysticism functions as a conceptual bridge, integrating diverse expressions across traditions.

Third, qualitative research complements quantitative studies by probing the content of mystical experiences and capturing phenomena beyond predefined categories. Semi-structured interviews designed to elicit the substance of mystical experience reveal a broader spectrum of experiential types than those typically identified in quantitative models. Some align closely with doctrinal frameworks. For instance, in a study with 139 Chinese Pure Land and Chan Buddhist monks and nuns, participants described the dissolution of selfhood not merely as consciousness of a void but as an intricate state of *zhenkong miaoyou* – "wondrous existence in true emptiness" (Chen et al., 2011). In another study with individuals in soulmate relationships, participants reported profound, self-effacing connections that extended beyond explicitly religious contexts (Chen & Patel, 2021). In a study with nineteen Daoist monastics, ego dissolution was interpreted through bodily sensations, such as the perception of energy movements (Chen et al., 2023). In a study with sixty-one trained shamans in North America, mysticism was understood as a fundamental shift in their perception of reality itself within the framework of Shamanic healing (Chen, 2023). More recently, in a study with thirty-nine Daoist monastics, mixed-methods and network analysis were used to examine the structure of their experiences, thereby refining the common core thesis within a less-studied tradition (Chen & Guo, 2025).

In sum, both theoretical argument and empirical evidence support the existence of a common experiential core of monistic mysticism, while allowing for variability in interpretive organization across traditions. Subtle differences emerge among samples from distinct religions, yet certain facets consistently define unitive mysticism, producing what Wittgenstein (1953) termed a "family resemblance" across traditions. This challenges the classical notion that all members of a category share a single essential feature. Instead, categories are linked by overlapping similarities, much like resemblances among family members who may share certain traits without any one being universally present. The modified common core thesis therefore, rests on three key elements: a universal experiential core at the facet level (e.g., ego loss), socially constructed variability at the factor level (e.g., introvertive factor), and stable family resemblances across cultural contexts. While monistic mysticism provides a valuable framework for understanding certain shared psychological phenomena, it has become increasingly evident that mysticism as a whole encompasses multiple forms of perceived reality, with ego dissolution representing but one among many possible configurations of selfhood.

3 Nondualistic Mysticism

The second layer, nondualistic mysticism, acknowledges the apparent duality and hierarchy between subject (e.g., the created, mundane existence) and object (e.g., a deity, God, or the cosmic order), while emphasizing the possibility that the created may ultimately become one with the Creator. It frequently takes the form of a numinous experience in which the world and humanity are perceived as imperfect reflections of an ultimate reality. Within this framework, mystical experiences often pursue detachment from the material and transient in order to return to the divine source – where unity with the divine is fully realized and the distinction between the created and the Creator dissolves. Nondualistic mysticism thus aligns with our definition of mysticism by affirming the existence of a transcendent reality beyond the mundane world and by requiring the subjugation of the individual self to an idealized manifestation of the divine. This form of mysticism incorporates a pursuit of universal principles inherent in monistic mysticism, insofar as many religious traditions strive for communion and oneness with ultimate reality. Yet it extends beyond monistic mysticism by recognizing that the individual is inherently distinct from the divine, such that the ultimate unity of the two is not assured or automatic.

Each religious tradition articulates its mystical experiences through distinct theological and philosophical languages, reflecting the uniqueness of its worldview. Determining the extent to which traditions converge on a shared mystical essence remains a significant challenge, precisely because of these differences. The following sections examine mystical thought within several major religious traditions as an entry point into deeper study. It is evident that such traditions cannot be neatly summed up, and what is presented here constitutes only approximations rather than exhaustive or axiomatic descriptions, leaving room for many exceptions. The section organizes these traditions according to their historical origins. The Abrahamic traditions, or People of the Book – Judaism, Christianity, and Islam – each develop distinctive mystical frameworks rooted in their monotheistic foundations. The Dharmic religions of Hinduism and Buddhism arise in India, with Buddhism extending beyond its homeland to take root in other cultures. In addition, two Chinese traditions, Daoism and Confucianism, are considered, offering perspectives that move outside a strictly monotheistic or theistic paradigm. The section concludes with a comparative discussion that reflects on the idea of "a religion of all religions" as a lens through which mysticism across traditions might be approached.

3.1 Abrahamic: Jewish, Christian, and Islamic Mysticism

3.1.1 Jewish Mysticism

Jewish mysticism is the pursuit of direct, experiential knowledge of God (Scholem, 1961), employing specific spiritual techniques to attain the unitive experience (Idel, 1988). In contrast to philosophical Judaism's emphasis on rationalism and abstraction, Jewish mysticism arises from a profound yearning to identify with the innermost divine essence of all things. Both the surface meaning, *nigleh* – the revealed aspect of an act or text, as exemplified in Jewish law and the Talmud – and the hidden matter, *nistar* – the mystical teachings of the Torah – are central to this mystical orientation. Jewish mysticism, therefore, entails the removal of outer coverings in order to disclose the inner quality of things (Weiner, 1969). Across history, Jewish spiritual thought and practice have developed through several distinct stages. The biblical period, particularly the book of Genesis, provides paradigmatic expressions of mystical doctrine and phenomena. The rabbinical era gave rise to Merkavah and Hekhalot mysticism, followed in the medieval period by the emergence of Kabbalah and, later, the flowering of Hasidism (Green, 1987). Scholem (1987) traces the origins of Kabbalah in twelfth-century Southern Europe to the text of the *Bahir*, culminating in the composition of the *Zohar*.

Several hallmarks define Jewish mysticism. A first is the perennial spiritual belief that "as above, so below," signifying a correspondence between divine order and mundane existence. Creation itself is understood as a process of divine emanation through the *Sefirot*, ten channels mediating between the physical world and *Ein Sof* – the infinite, unknowable aspect of God that transcends human comprehension (Idel, 1988). This dynamic interplay between heavenly power and earthly existence unfolds in two contrasting mystical models: the anabatic ascent, in which the mystic rises upward to bring down divine power, and the katabatic descent, wherein Messiahs enter into the realm of evil to redeem fallen souls (Idel, 2013).

Another defining feature is the emphasis on action. For the Jewish mystic, mystical union requires the performance of precise rituals, rather than a passive reception of divine grace, as is often the case in Christianity. In this respect, Jewish mysticism shares with Hindu mysticism an emphasis on ritual, on its cosmic effects, and on the use of breathing techniques to induce altered states of consciousness (Idel, 2013). This emphasis is further accentuated by the insistence on precision in mystical techniques – whether ecstatic, theurgical, or talismanic (Idel, 1995) – since their efficacy depends on meticulous execution. Moreover, many of these practices are not regarded as mere human inventions but as divine revelations, reinforcing nomianism, or strict adherence to divine commandments, as central to religious faith and practice.

Finally, as in many other mystical traditions, Jewish mysticism often embraces paradox. The supreme, most sacred spiritual reality is ineffable, and God remains ultimately beyond human comprehension (Idel, 1995). Because Jewish theology preserves the fundamental distinction between Creator and creation, mystical self-loss or merging with the divine is exceedingly rare. As Scholem (1961, pp. 122–123) observes, "It is only in extremely rare cases that ecstasy signifies actual union with God, in which the individuality abandons itself to the rapture of complete submersion in the divine stream. Even in this ecstatic frame of mind, the Jewish mystic almost invariably retains a sense of the distance between the Creator and His creature." This paradox – the simultaneous longing for and impossibility of full union – may account for the Jewish mystic's intense focus on text (Torah) and language (Hebrew). The Hebrew language and alphabet are considered sacred, serving as direct expressions of divine thought. Jewish mysticism extends beyond the meaning of words to the very form of letters themselves, inspiring spiritual techniques such as gematria, in which numerical values are assigned to words to uncover hidden connections. Through the practice of gematria, the mystic undergoes a psychological shift that enables a closer approach to divine reality.

3.1.2 Christian Mysticism

Rather than "mystical union," Christian mysticism is better described as beliefs and practices centered on the direct "presence of God." In his magnum opus, McGinn argues that mystics seek to understand and live daily life in God's presence. His historical survey of Christian mysticism begins with its origins through the fifth century (McGinn, 1991) and extends to quietism in seventeenth-century southern Europe (McGinn, 2021). Additionally, McGinn (2006) has edited key writings on Christian mysticism, providing firsthand accounts and annotations that highlight mysticism as a transformative encounter with God's presence rather than an abstract theological concept.

The emphasis on experience was not widespread in early Christianity. Before the twelfth century, monastic mystics rarely spoke of personal encounters with God, instead expressing mystical transformation through biblical exegesis. With Bernard of Clairvaux, active in the first half of the twelfth century, personal experience became more pronounced, culminating in what McGinn (1998) calls the "flowering of mysticism" through the sixteenth century. Figures like Meister Eckhart (2009) preached the unity of the soul with the divine, famously stating, "The eye with which I see God is the same eye with which God sees me: my eye and God's eye are one eye, one seeing, one knowing, and one love" (Sermon 57, p. 298). Similarly, Teresa of Ávila (1979) described her spiritual journey through the metaphor of an inner castle with seven mansions, representing stages of growth and intimacy with God. At its core lies the innermost chamber, where God resides and where the ultimate Spiritual Marriage occurs.

McGinn (2013) outlines three key characteristics of Christian mysticism. First, orthodoxy holds greater importance than orthopraxy. The doctrines of the Trinity (Father, Son, and Holy Spirit) and Jesus Christ as the Messiah distinguish Christian mysticism from other Abrahamic traditions, despite the diversity of Christological interpretations within it. Second, Christian mysticism emphasizes action. The balance between mystical experience and its visible effects is framed as the relationship between contemplation and active love. Charity is often seen as more vital to the Church than personal ecstasy. The highest mystical goal is to achieve a state where one actively loves in the midst of contemplation, exemplified by Ignatius of Loyola, founder of the Jesuits. Finally, Christian mysticism is communal. While individuals prepare for union with God through mystical teachings, this experience often occurs within the Church's communal life – through biblical reading, liturgy, sacraments, prayer, and preaching. The knowledge gained through mysticism is considered a divine gift, meant not for personal enlightenment alone but for the service of the Church through teaching, intercession, and healing.

3.1.3 Islamic Mysticism

Islamic mysticism is most often expressed in the form of *tasawwuf* or Sufism, which is rooted in the Qur'an and Sunnah. Central to Sufi thought are the principles of *tawhid* (divine unity), the transformative power of *dhikr* (remembrance of God), and the integration of inner virtues with outward practices modeled on the life of the Prophet Muhammad (Nasr, 1991). Within the Sufi framework, three interrelated concepts structure the mystical path: *shariah*, the code of conduct that governs Muslim life; *haqiqah*, the knowledge of ultimate reality attained through communion with God; and *tariqah*, the path that bridges the exoteric *shariah* with the esoteric *haqiqah*. These three form a symbolic architecture: *shariah* as the circumference, *haqiqah* as the center, and *tariqah* as the radii connecting the two (Guenon, 2009). In this vision, external observance, inner realization, and the spiritual path remain inseparable dimensions of mystical life.

The principle of *tawhid*, or the oneness of God, stands at the very heart of Islamic mysticism. Yet Sufis have historically offered diverse interpretations of how this unity should be approached and to what extent the human being can draw near to God (Fakhry, 2004). Neoplatonic philosophers such as al-Farabi, Ibn Sina, and Ibn Bajjah emphasized reason and intellectual contemplation as the primary means of comprehending God, advancing the human intellect as a path toward divine knowledge. By contrast, early Sufi figures such as Junayd of Baghdad and later al-Ghazali articulated a more dualistic vision in which God is approached through awe, reverence, and love, yet without intimacy or identification. In more radical voices, such as al-Hallaj and al-Bastami, this boundary dissolved, leading to bold proclamations of identity with the divine. Rumi, meanwhile, celebrated the transformative power of love, music, poetry, and dance, emphasizing the ecstatic dimensions of mystical union (Lewis, 2000). Expanding upon these currents, Ibn Arabi articulated a sweeping metaphysical system in which all differences and otherness are dissolved in God, positing creation as nothing other than the Creator's self-disclosure. Since Ibn Arabi, the path to true gnosis has often been conceived as a progression from the illusion of separateness to the realization that all existence is one with the Divine (Awn, 2013).

Although the unity of God ultimately eludes empirical verification and rational demonstration, it may nonetheless be discerned through layers of manifestation, each of which serves as a sign of divine oneness (Schimmel, 1994). One way in which these signs are recognized is through the cultivation of the creative imagination, particularly through meditation and contemplative practice. Such exercises allow the seeker to perceive unity beneath the multiplicity of the world, thereby recognizing creation as an interconnected field of divine self-disclosure. It is in this light that Ibn Arabi develops the notion of the *alam al-mithal*, or the Imaginal World, an intermediate realm where spiritual realities assume symbolic forms and physical realities become spiritualized. In this realm, divine energies manifest in ways accessible to human perception, while never losing their essential transcendence. Imagination thus becomes not a faculty of idle fantasy but a bridge between thought and being, a means of accessing divine realities directly and facilitating the soul's ascent toward union with God (Corbin, 1969).

3.2 Dharmic: Hindu and Buddhist Mysticism

3.2.1 Hindu Mysticism

One classical way to understand the progression of Hindu mysticism is as a journey from the *Vedas* to the *Upanishads*, and finally through the *Bhagavad Gita*. The journey begins with the vision of the four Vedas, emphasizing cosmic unity and divine order, followed by an exploration of sacrifice and ritual as a means of connecting with the divine. The Upanishadic quest deepens this inquiry, seeking ultimate reality (*Brahman*) and self-realization (*atman*), while the *Bhagavad Gita* integrates devotion (*bhakti yoga*), knowledge (*jnana yoga*), and action (*karma yoga*) into a comprehensive spiritual path. *Yoga*, meaning "to yoke" or "to unite," in its narrow sense refers to the Yoga school – one of the six orthodox systems of Hindu philosophy – which developed with relative independence from the other traditions and could thus be flexibly absorbed into diverse mystical practices. More broadly, yoga encompasses any spiritual discipline – meditation, breath control, concentration – that unites the seeker with their ultimate quest for liberation (Eliade, 1958). The richness of Hindu philosophies is often expressed through myths and symbols, employing motifs such as the lotus, wheel, and serpent to articulate truths otherwise beyond expression (Zimmer, 1946).

Hindu mysticism may be traced across several overlapping phases (Sharma, 2013). The earliest form, sometimes called acosmic mysticism, involves direct illumination without deity worship, exemplified by Samkhya and classical Yoga. Lacking a clear conception of God, the yogin does not seek personal union with a divine presence but rather the realization of the self in its pure, isolated state, freed from the entanglements of material nature. A subsequent phase of theistic mysticism emerges with figures such as Ramanuja and Madhva, who affirm *Brahman* as both the indwelling ground of the universe and the source of all souls. For Ramanuja, *Brahman* is the immanent reality in which human souls and the cosmos exist as the body of God, yet remain distinct, wholly dependent on Him for their being. Parallel to these developments, the *bhakti* tradition expands the mystical landscape through devotional paths centered on personal, relational encounters with God, expressed through love, surrender, and ecstatic union with *saguna* (qualified, personal) Brahman. This devotional current crystallized around deities such as Krishna, Shiva, and the Goddess, and profoundly shaped the emotional and communal dimensions of mystical life in Hinduism.

Finally, absolutist mysticism, most forcefully articulated by Shankara's Advaita Vedanta, "the end of the Vedas," interprets the *Upanishads* as teaching that *Brahman* is without attributes (*nirguna*), infinite, and the sole truth of existence (Sivaraman, 1989). In this view, bondage (*samsara*) and liberation (*moksha*) are mere illusions born of ignorance, since the *atman* is ever one with *Brahman*. Yet Advaita also recognizes the provisional significance of *saguna Brahman*, the personal God, as an object of worship and meditation, preparing aspirants for the eventual realization of formless *nirguna Brahman*. Shankara (1947) thus states, "How can one imagine duality in Brahman, which is entire like the ether, without a second, the supreme reality? There is neither birth nor death, neither bound nor aspiring soul, neither liberated soul nor seeker after liberation – this is the ultimate and absolute truth" (p. 115). Another significant strand is Tantric mysticism, which arose in medieval India and emphasized ritual, mantra, subtle-body practices, and the harnessing of divine energy (*shakti*) to achieve transcendence. Unlike the renunciatory tendencies of classical Advaita, Tantra often affirms the sacredness of the body and the dynamic, creative power of the divine manifest in material existence. Modern figures such as Ramakrishna (Nikhilananda, 1942) and Sri Aurobindo (1990), who have both influenced and been influenced by the West, further elucidated left-handed and right-handed Tantra – integrating the erotic and mystical – and transforming ritual practices into internal contemplative exercises.

Across these mystical traditions, Hinduism emphasizes right action (orthopraxy) rather than right belief (orthodoxy), in contrast to Christian mysticism. A Hindu must fulfill their *varnasrama dharma* – duty (*dharma*) determined by caste (*varna*) and stage of life (*ashrama*). Thus, Hinduism's ritual precision and caste-based restrictions stand in stark contrast to its doctrinal inclusivity, accommodating nontheism, theism, absolutism, and syncretism (Zimmer, 1951). By contrast, Jainism and Buddhism reverse the emphasis: while Hinduism prescribes worldly duty under Brahmanic supervision, Jain and Buddhist traditions champion renunciation, as exemplified in the figures of Mahavira and the Buddha (Dumont, 1975).

In yoga, a dialectical tension exists between effort and surrender. Terms such as *vitarka* (inquiry) and *vicara* (analysis) indicate a mind engaged in self-examination. At first, this deliberation directs attention to the movements of thought; later, in advanced meditation, such cognitive activity dissolves into an unbroken flow of awareness. The *Yoga Sutra* teaches that this state is not achieved by forceful suppression or overanalyzing thoughts – which merely introduce new waves of mental activity – but through detachment (Staal, 1975). This paradox is often misunderstood, leading some to misinterpret yoga as passive or inactive. On the contrary, the true yogin is vigorous, disciplined, and engaged, possibly even while living fully within the world.

3.2.2 Buddhist Mysticism

The Upanishads, especially the *Chandogya*, frame spiritual experience in terms of union, affirming the nonduality of Atman and Brahman. In contrast, Buddhism emphasizes *shunyata* – emptiness or nothingness – wherein the self dissolves into the nullity of all things (Paper, 2004). Among the most influential philosophical traditions is Nagarjuna's *Madhyamaka* (Middle Way), which profoundly shaped Buddhist thought and later became foundational for many tantric systems (Zimmer, 1951). The earliest transmission of Indian Buddhism to Sri Lanka and later Southeast Asia gave rise to Theravada, a tradition that stresses mindfulness, monastic discipline, and ethical living as the basis for liberation (Takeuchi, 1993). The foundational teachings of the Buddha, preserved in the Pali Canon, remain central to this tradition (Bhikkhu Bodhi, 2005). Even earlier, in the Tibetan cultural sphere, the indigenous Zhangzhung Bön religion flourished, and while it later absorbed Buddhist elements, its mystical corpus exhibits less reliance on Hindu tantric influences than Vajrayana Buddhism (Norbu, 2013).

Buddhism entered China in the first century CE, where it encountered Daoism and Confucianism, giving rise to distinctive East Asian forms of Mahayana (Takeuchi, 1999). Chinese *Chan* (later *Zen* in Japan) emphasized the immediacy of awakening and practical enlightenment integrated into daily life. This syncretic spirit extended into Korea, where Buddhism blended with indigenous shamanic beliefs, and into Japan, where Zen and Pure Land practices developed into highly distinct currents. A central feature of Zen is the seamless integration of spiritual realization and practical activity, embodied in the Japanese concept of *satori* (enlightenment). *Satori* represents a sudden, transformative experience of oneness and spontaneity, in which the duality between self and world dissolves. Zen masters often described this as the essence of spirituality itself: an uncompromising engagement with the immediacy of life. The Japanese term *myo* (Chinese: *miao*) conveys this ineffable quality, denoting "a mode of activity which comes directly out of one's inmost self without being intercepted by the dichotomous intellect" (Suzuki, 1959, p. 140).

Buddhism formally entered Tibet in the eighth century, where it developed into Vajrayana, the "Diamond Vehicle." Vajrayana emphasizes the transformative power of tantra (*tantra* in Sanskrit meaning "thread" or "weaving"), while in Tibet the term *gyud* (continuum) reflects the recognition of an inherent Buddha-nature present in all beings (Blofeld, 1970). Vajrayana is characterized by its elaborate system of nine vehicles (*yanas*), each providing progressive methods toward enlightenment (Dudjom Rinpoche, 1991). Entry into tantric practice requires initiation by a qualified guru through ritual empowerments (*dbang*), and unwavering devotion to the teacher is considered indispensable. The guru is often perceived as an embodiment of enlightenment itself, capable of awakening the disciple through direct transmission, "like a lamp lighting another lamp." A classical account of these foundations is found in *The Words of My Perfect Teacher* (Kunzang Lama, 1993).

Tantric practice proceeds in two major stages. In the Generation Stage, practitioners cultivate deity visualization, transforming ordinary perception into awakened vision. By visualizing oneself as a deity (*yidam*) and inhabiting its enlightened qualities, the yogin integrates body, speech, and mind with the divine archetype, aided by mantras, mandalas, and ritual symbolism. The celebrated mantra *Om Mani Padme Hum* epitomizes this devotional and transformative practice (Govinda, 1969). In the Completion Stage, practitioners engage in subtle-body yogas, manipulating vital winds (*tsa lung*) and cultivating inner heat (*tummo*) to deepen realization and directly experience the nature of mind (Blofeld, 1970).

As the pinnacle of the Nyingma school's teachings, *Dzogchen* ("Great Perfection") emphasizes direct recognition of the mind's true nature (*rigpa*). Dudjom Lingpa's visionary teachings describe awareness as inherently pure (*kadag*) and spontaneously present (*lhun grub*), transcending conceptual elaboration. Dzogchen practice involves meditative absorption, self-liberation from mental obscurations, and cultivating nondual awareness, revealing the natural state of primordial consciousness (Wallace, 2015).

In Vajrayana, mystical transmission often unfolds through esoteric revelation. Teachings may be concealed by enlightened beings and later rediscovered by visionary masters known as *tertons* (treasure revealers). These revealed texts, or *terma*, often appear in visions, dreams, or meditative states, ensuring the continuity of wisdom across generations (Gyatso, 1998). Such transmissions are sometimes linked to subtle-body channels, resonating with Daoist internal alchemy and tantric physiology. In this way, Buddhist mysticism situates the individual within a vast temporal and cosmic continuum, in which liberation unfolds across lifetimes, mediated by direct transmissions of wisdom and the recognition of the luminous, nondual nature of reality.

3.3 Chinese: Daoist and Confucian Mysticism

3.3.1 Daoist Mysticism

Grounded in Chinese cosmology, which posits the oneness of the universe and its natural rhythms, the Daoist mystical endeavor seeks not only to restore cosmic harmony but also to attain realization – to "make heaven and earth his body" (Kohn, 2013). One of the core Daoist mystical ideals is tranquility and nonaction (*wuwei*). However, *wuwei* is not passive acceptance; rather, it arises through profound mystical cultivation, aligning an individual with the rhythms of the cosmos. Early Daoists – Laozi and Zhuangzi – through specific practices such as sitting in oblivion (*zuowang*), may have achieved a transformation in which the self dissolves into a unitive mystical experience of merging with the Way (*Dao*). Following this transcendence, when adepts return to worldly engagement, their consciousness is radically transformed, allowing them to "do nothing yet leave nothing undone" (*wuwei er wubuwei*). This suggests that original Daoism may have consisted of one or more master-disciple lineages centered on the contemplative practice of inner cultivation. This practice formed the distinctive techniques (*shu*) around which these lineages coalesced and from which they ultimately derived their identities (Roth, 2021).

Beyond this deeply abstract ideal of unity with the *Dao*, Daoism's unique spiritual insight lies in its equal emphasis on body and spirit as integral to spiritual transformation. Foundational to Daoist thought is the concept of *qi* – the vital energy that flows through the body's meridians, akin to blood circulating through the veins. This focus on the body originated in early Daoist external alchemy, where practitioners sought physical immortality through elixirs composed of minerals and medicinal herbs. By the sixth century, the emphasis shifted inward, giving rise to internal alchemy (*neidan*), wherein the body itself became the locus of spiritual transformation. The cultivation of the three treasures – *jing* (essence), *qi* (vital energy), and *shen* (spirit) – became central to this practice. Zhang Boduan, founder of the Southern Neidan School, outlined a three-stage process in his *Wuzhen Pian* ("Awakening to Reality"; Pregadio, 2009): refining *jing* into *qi*, refining *qi* into *shen*, and refining *shen* to return to primordial emptiness. This interplay between *jing* and *qi* sustains life (*ming*), while *shen* defines one's spiritual nature (*xing*). Wang Chongyang, founder of the Northern Quanzhen School, articulated this dynamic in the 11th discourse of his *Fifteen Discourses to Establish the Teachings*: "Spiritual nature (*xing*) is spirit (*shen*); life (*ming*) is *qi*. Spirit and life intertwine, like a bird riding the wind."

Given the essential role of bodily energies, Daoism emphasizes the joint cultivation of body and spirit – *xing ming shuangxiu*. Cultivating *ming* entails nurturing *qi* through breathing exercises, meditation, and a tranquil lifestyle, while cultivating *xing* involves aligning oneself with the *Dao*, fostering inner harmony, and refining the mind and spirit. The philosophy of *xing ming shuangxiu* rests on the equilibrium between these two aspects, as Daoists maintain that physical life (*ming*) and spiritual nature (*xing*) are interdependent. Practices that cultivate both spirit and body are indispensable for harmonizing with the *Dao* and, ultimately, for achieving immortality (Kohn, 1993).

3.3.2 Confucian Mysticism

Confucian ideals align closely with Daoist thought in their shared focus on *xing* (spiritual nature) and *Dao* (the Way). The Confucian canon, *Zhongyong* ("Doctrine of the Mean"), begins by stating: "What Heaven has conferred upon people is called spiritual nature; to follow this nature is called the Way; and aligning one's nature with the Way is called self-cultivation." This mystical process of self-cultivation (*xiushen*) fosters a deep connection with others, nature, and Heaven, as illustrated in *Daxue* ("The Greater Learning"): a cultivated self leads to the regulation of the family, which in turn enables the governance of the state and ultimately the harmonization of everything under Heaven.

The goal of self-cultivation is twofold. From a pragmatic perspective, it culminates in the ideal of the "inner sage, outer king" (*neisheng waiwang*), wherein the cultivation of personal virtue, wisdom, and moral character enables one to govern society and lead others effectively (Zhang, 2009). On a higher level, it aspires toward the "unity of Heaven and humanity" (*tianren heyi*), reflecting the profound interconnectedness between humans and the cosmos. This mystical ideal is realized through the alignment of human nature with the cosmic order, achieved via self-cultivation and moral virtuosity (Kohn, 2013).

Mystical union in Confucianism entails transcending self-centeredness to embody *ren* (benevolence) and *cheng* (authenticity). *Ren* is the principle of love – "The *ren* person loves others," as stated concisely in *Mencius* (*Li Lou II*). *Cheng* represents authenticity attained through deep self-reflection – "All things are already complete in me. There is no greater delight than becoming aware of my authenticity through self-examination" (*Mencius, Jin Xin I*). By embodying these principles, one undergoes genuine spiritual transformation and applies benevolent ideals to effect positive change in the world (Tu & Tucker, 2003).

Unlike other religious traditions, Confucianism does not emphasize deity devotion or meditative practices. However, it has maintained an unbroken tradition of self-cultivation through the study of classical texts and the words of sages. Neo-Confucianist Xiong Shili (1945) argues that the *Six Classics* provide timeless guidance for aligning human behavior with cosmic order and achieving moral clarity. He advocates for the method of "interpreting the classics through oneself," urging readers to adapt ancient wisdom to contemporary challenges while preserving its ethical core. This process ultimately realizes the principle of "the unity of essence and function" (*tiyong bu'er*), wherein spiritual transformation serves as the foundation for benefiting the world (Xiong, 1932). These twin aims – self-transcendence and moral application – have remained central to Confucian values across generations.

3.4 Comparative Religious Perspective

This brief review of mystical approaches across various religious traditions suggests that they impart diverse systems of truth, each often claiming exclusivity. While different religions emerge within specific temporal and cultural contexts as adaptations to particular social realities, they are not entirely isolated from one another. Instead, they exist within a broader history of mutual influence and exchange. For instance, Sufism should not be viewed as an isolated mystical strand within Islam but rather as an integral component of the broader Islamic tradition, one that has also absorbed syncretic influences from Hindu and Buddhist traditions (Ernst, 1997). Such syncretism is even more pronounced in the Chinese traditions (Chen & Guo, in press). Likewise, the monistic mysticism, with its focus on unity devoid of content, has been shaped by a lineage that traces through Hekhalot mysticism, Gnosticism, medieval Kabbalah, Sufism, and Hindu and Buddhist traditions before returning to modern Hindu interpretations (Michaelson, 2011).

The human potential for transcendence is realized through social processes that lead to the construction of objective worldviews, the articulation of sacred universes, and, under certain conditions, the institutional specialization of religions (Luckmann, 1967). Different religious traditions give concrete form to shared mythological motifs, such as the distinction between the sacred and the profane, where the sacred represents transcendent, eternal realities that give life meaning, while the profane encompasses the mundane, everyday world. Myths, symbols, and rituals function as bridges between these two realms, allowing individuals to connect with the sacred and situate themselves within a meaningful cosmic order (Eliade, 1959). Similarly, creation myths, sacred time and space, and rituals of renewal appear in various traditions, fulfilling analogous existential needs (Eliade, 1954). These recurring themes are systematically explored in Eliade's encyclopedic *History of Religious Ideas* (1978–1985). It takes scholars such as Joseph Campbell (1959–1968) to reveal how myths function as mediators between humanity and the mysteries of existence, frequently expressed through festivals and sacrifices that unify individuals with the sacred. Myths, as Campbell suggests, serve as cultural "masks" for universal truths, rooted in shared psychological archetypes, and reflect humanity's ongoing quest to understand existence and its mysteries.

On both sides of the Atlantic, the comparative religions movement has flourished, marked by the establishment of Eranos in the 1930s, centered around Carl G. Jung (Hakl, 2014), and its American counterpart, Esalen, founded in the 1960s, which played a central role in the subsequent human potential movement (Kripal, 2008). This interdisciplinary study of religion and mysticism leads to the conclusion that mystical traditions often achieve similar outcomes through three primary means: the deconstruction of social conditioning, the abandonment of dualistic thinking, and the dissolution of essentialism (Watts, 1961).

Religious experiences, or what we term "nondualistic mysticism" in this section, thus present a compelling case for the idea that ostensibly distinct and outwardly conflicting doctrinal claims may, in esoteric understanding, share a great deal in common: a unified reality that inherently transcends all apparent contradictions. This perspective does not advocate for an indiscriminate syncretic fusion of traditions, nor does it dismiss the undeniable diversity of dogmas and rituals across the world's religions. Rather, as Cutsinger (1997) eloquently states, "Truth does not negate forms from an external standpoint, but rather transcends them from within" (p. 198).

4 Dualistic Mysticism

The third layer is dualistic mysticism, wherein a spiritual realm is encountered as a separate and contrasting reality to the human world. This duality implies a clear division between the subjective self and the perceived realities, and it is the encounter and interaction of the two that marks the nature of dualistic mysticism. In these experiences, the perceiver retains individuality, unlike the dissolving selfhood found in the previous two types of mysticism. Dualistic mysticism aligns with the definition of mysticism by acknowledging a reality that starkly opposes the physical realm, involving the transformation of the ego to engage with spiritual beings. This form of mysticism also contains elements of nondualistic mysticism, since spirits are often perceived as possessing higher wisdom and power, and the spiritual realm is regarded as more fundamental than the physical reality. At the same time, dualistic mysticism hints at certain universal principles associated with monistic mysticism, as the unitive vision of the self and cosmos is sometimes expressed as a human universal.

This section explores encounters with nonhuman forms of consciousness and intelligence, focusing primarily on spirits that inhabit spiritual realms distinct from the human world. The first part begins with American Indigenous traditions, many of which include the practice of shamanism, characterized by journeys into spiritual realms and interactions with guides for healing purposes. The second part discusses Spiritism, highlighting its unique approaches to engaging with spiritual entities and extending to the implications of unidentified flying object (UFO) sightings for encounters with nonhuman intelligence. The third part considers psychedelic experiences, which offer a means for expanding consciousness and connecting with the nonmaterial world, providing transformative encounters outside traditional shamanic contexts. The final part examines esotericism and related traditions that strive for a unitive vision of eternal truths, often grounded in wisdom perceived as originating from spiritual realms.

The goal here is not to confine particular traditions within a single type of mysticism, nor to reduce the variety of experiences to rigid categories. Psychedelic encounters, for instance, often include elements of monistic mysticism, such as ego dissolution, while many Native American traditions also involve practices that lean toward nondualistic experiences. The examples presented are thus prototypical, intended to provide wide coverage of religious and spiritual traditions without denying the overlapping and multifaceted nature of mystical experience.

4.1 American Indigenous Traditions and Shamanism

The American Indigenous people comprise culturally and linguistically diverse groups, generally divided geographically into North, Meso, and South America. While spiritual practices vary greatly from tribe to tribe, common threads form a continuum of body, kinship, land, and cosmos (Grim, 2013). First, there is a strong land attachment. Native wisdom asserts that just as individuals depend on their nurturing society, so too do humans rely on the sustaining earth. Long-term inhabitation of bioregions fosters spiritual union with specific terrains, animals, plants, and geological features, cultivating a deep sense of localized spiritual belonging.

Closely related to land attachment is kinship with cosmological powers. Mystical knowledge in American indigenous traditions emerges from individual experiences in dialogue with community mythic norms and contemplative encounters with regional ecologies. Personal spiritual revelations often come through visions and dreams, received from deities who are considered ancestors or become kin to the visionary. This continuity – from individual to ancestral lineage – reflects the belief that one's personal story contains the whole of the collective, much like a holographic film, where any aspect of one's life can manifest the sacred mystery in its entirety.

Finally, the individual is also the body. Rituals, mythic narratives, and cosmological visions express embodied spiritual realities, often correlating the human form with bioregional features like mountains, rivers, and forests. Local species further expand this correlative cosmology, establishing somatic correspondences as visionary ideals for personal maturation. With these foundational elements in place, a review of the three regions follows.

North American (commonly referred to as Native American) mysticism is rooted in the belief that the sacred is immanent in the natural world – an Earth-centered mysticism emphasizing immersion in nature's spiritual energies and recognizing the divine within all creation. Visions, often achieved through fasting, isolation, or ceremonies, are central to Native American mysticism, serving both personal and communal purposes by offering guidance and power (Hultkrantz, 1987). Medicine men or shamanic healers act as intermediaries, attaining healing power with the help of guardian spirits to communicate with the supernatural on behalf of their communities (Hultkrantz, 1979). In gathering-hunting traditions, each member was expected to cultivate a personal relationship with guardian spirits to ensure survival and fulfill communal responsibilities.

Mesoamerican traditions emphasize the *axis mundi*, a symbolic link between the heavens, earth, and underworld, integrating time and space as sacred dimensions. Pre-Columbian religions such as those of the Nahua and Maya sought to harmonize human existence with cosmic forces through rituals, myths, and deities like Quetzalcoatl, the Plumed Serpent, who bridged earthly and divine realms. The arrival of Spanish Catholicism introduced syncretism, blending Indigenous practices with Christian elements, such as the reinterpretation of the world tree as the cross and the veneration of the Virgin of Guadalupe (Gossen & León-Portilla, 1993). The traditional use of psychoactive plants, such as *peyote*, for spiritual and ceremonial purposes is well documented (Schultes et al., 1992).

South American traditions have drawn significant scholarly attention for their use of *ayahuasca*, a psychoactive brew made from *Banisteriopsis caapi* vine and *Psychotria viridis* leaves, used in ceremonies to induce altered states of consciousness (Metzner, 2006). Among Amazonian Tucano communities, ayahuasca serves as a bridge to the supernatural, facilitating encounters with spirit beings that offer healing and wisdom (Reichel-Dolmatoff, 1978). Not all ayahuasca-induced spirit encounters are voluntary; some initiates report unexpected spirit callings that grant healing abilities (Apffel-Marglin & Gonzales, 2022). Western-trained scientists have also provided anecdotal accounts of ayahuasca experiences. A Canadian biologist described gaining direct knowledge of molecular structures by "becoming" the plant in a visionary trip (Narby, 1999), while a medical doctor attested to its role in facilitating profound psychiatric emotional release (Tafur, 2017). Psychological analyses have explored ayahuasca's effects on personal transformation (Shanon, 2002), and research on Santo Daime, a Brazilian ayahuasca tradition, highlights mediumistic experiences in which suffering spirits are channeled through the bodies of practitioners (Barnard, 2022).

Across these regions, the shaman plays a pivotal role in facilitating rituals, healing, and spiritual journeys. While the term "shaman" originates from Tungusic language groups of Central Asia, shamanic practices exhibit striking similarities worldwide. The belief in a spirit-inhabited realm and the practice of theurgy – rituals invoking divine presence – have been central to diverse human societies for centuries (Eliade, 1964). Neurological research suggests a biological basis for shamanic practices, linking them to the brain's reptilian, paleomammalian, and neomammalian layers, each governing distinct behavioral, emotional, and cognitive functions (MacLean, 1990). Studies point to a neuroanatomical foundation involving dopamine activity in ventromedial cortical areas, supporting a common basis for altered states of consciousness in both shamanism and other spiritual traditions (Previc, 2009; Winkelman, 2010).

The classical techniques of inducing ecstatic consciousness – such as visualization and rhythmic drumming – have been adapted into a structured set of practices accessible to modern practitioners (Harner, 1980). Shamanic techniques have led many Western practitioners to report encounters with a nonordinary reality, suggesting a common human capacity to access spiritual dimensions that are distinct from the physical reality (Harner, 2013). Regardless of the ontological validity of such experiences, the spiritual domains where shamans navigate for healing purposes maintain functional validity.

However, caution is necessary in interpreting Indigenous spirituality through the *etic* (outsider) perspectives, as they may overlook core Indigenous epistemologies. These traditions often operate within *perspectivism*, the idea that nonhuman beings perceive reality from their own subjective perspectives, rather than being observed by human observers. This perspective contrasts with Western dualisms of human versus nonhuman or observer versus observed. Understanding the spiritual world, therefore, requires becoming the observed rather than merely analyzing it from an outsider's perspective (Viveiros de Castro, 2014). As in Amazonian ayahuasca traditions, drinking the plant, and therefore merging with it, is the only viable way to receive its wisdom.

4.2 Spiritist Encounters

Encountering spirits or other nonhuman immaterial entities is a common feature in Shamanism and mediumistic practices across human cultures. These experiences can be both active and passive. In spirit possession, the individual being possessed often displays a different personality, losing their original identity and acting involuntarily (Myers, 1903). This occurs in both actively sought possessions, such as those by deities in Daoist and folk religious traditions in Taiwan (Jordan & Overmyer, 1986), Southeast Asia (Watson & Ellen, 1993), Australian Aboriginal cultures (Elkin, 1977), and African traditions (Elkin, 1977; Olupona, 2000), as well as in passive receptions of spirits. In Shamanic trance, shamans access spirit power, receiving guidance and healing methods from spiritual guides. Unlike passive possession, shamans typically retain awareness and volition, distinguishing Shamanic ecstasy from spirit possession. These spiritist encounters are not confined to isolated religious activities but are deeply woven into everyday life, influencing social structures, governance, and communal well-being.

It is not uncommon to encounter uncanny or malevolent spirits in dreams. These entities, often perceived as demons or lowly beings with consciousness, are not arbitrary; they serve important psychological functions when properly understood. The Senoi people, for instance, prescribe confronting and battling dream demons until their terror and mischief are dissolved (Van Eeden, 1913). The Senoi believe that, with communal support, individuals can confront, control, and harness all entities and energies within the dream realm, emerging from these encounters with enhanced character and emotional strength. This process taps into the innermost self, where mental processes are least constrained by external factors and guided by inherent balancing mechanisms. Sleep, as the most unrestricted form of mental exploration, becomes a space for societal recognition of dreams, affirming individual acceptance (Stewart, 1972).

Numerous theories have emerged regarding the realm of spirits, many of which imply a dualistic existence encompassing both human and nonhuman entities. Allan Kardec (1857) established Spiritism in nineteenth-century France, synthesizing teachings received from spirits through mediums into a structured doctrine. His *Spiritist Book*, comprising over 1,000 questions and answers, addresses topics such as the immortality of the soul, reincarnation, moral laws, and humanity's ultimate destiny. Kardec presents the spiritual world as the primary and eternal reality, with the physical world being secondary and transient. Spirits are described as immaterial beings that evolve through reincarnation, progressing morally and intellectually across lifetimes toward eventual purification and union with the divine. Spirits are hierarchically classified based on their moral and intellectual development, ranging from impure to pure spirits. Reincarnation serves as a mechanism for spiritual growth, with each life offering opportunities to learn and overcome imperfections. Similar, though less systematic, theories discuss connections between reincarnation and models of the soul through alleged personal experiences (Semkiw, 2011). Additionally, manuals like those by Dominguez (2008) explore the nature of spiritual entities – such as spirit guides, ancestors, ghosts, angels, and divine beings – and how humans can interact with them for guidance, healing, and personal growth. It is emphasized that these entities exist in different realms of consciousness and can be accessed through intentional practices like meditation, ritual, and divination.

Despite these theories and anecdotal accounts, the metaphysical status of the spiritual realm and its relationship to the physical world remains subtle and porous. After his first ecstatic flight on the psychoactive devil's weed, Castaneda asked Don Juan, a Yaqui shaman, whether his body had actually flown or if it was merely his imagination. Don Juan replied that he flew as one is *supposed* to fly on devil's weed, and third-person consensus could be achieved if others understood this. Unsatisfied with this elusive response, Castaneda persisted in his dualistic view, suggesting, "If I had tied myself to a rock with a heavy chain, I would have flown just the same, because my body had nothing to do with my flying." Don Juan responded with incredulity, almost ridiculing the idea: "If you tie yourself to a rock, ... I'm afraid you will have to fly holding the rock with its heavy chain" (Castaneda, 1968, p. 102). This exchange highlights how our perception is accustomed to evaluating reality in physical terms, often using physicality as the primary criterion for what is "real" or illusory. Yet, reality may encompass both the real and the non-physically real.

The phenomenon of UFOs further illustrates this point. While many report physical experiences with UFOs – ranging from sightings to alien abductions – there remains no irrefutable physical evidence, such as a publicly accessible object to touch. Unidentified flying objects often materialize and dematerialize at will, synchronizing with the subjective states of witnesses, which complicates their classification as mere "objects." Moreover, their maneuvers defy basic laws of flight, rendering terms like "flying" equally suspect. Simply put, UFOs are neither objects nor flying in the conventional sense (Vallée, 1991).

Recognizing the nonphysical nature of UFO encounters expands our understanding of this phenomenon. Instead of asking where UFOs come from in space, we might also ask where they come from in time. Vallée (1991) suggests they could even originate from our own future. The key to the UFO phenomenon lies in its psychic effects. Much like dreams, UFO accounts are highly symbolic, pointing to something beyond themselves. They often possess the quality of dreams while also manifesting as physical events.

Unidentified flying objects have appeared throughout human history, always manifesting in ways that align with the cultural and temporal context of their witnesses. Hancock (2006) suggests that spirits coevolve with human society, appearing as apparitions or even extraterrestrial beings to align with contemporary understanding. This implies that one or many nonphysical, spiritual realms may coexist with the physical human realm, making encounters inevitable. The recently developed concept of panentheism further supports this idea, arguing that God – or spirit – is both immanent (present within the world) and transcendent (existing beyond it). Panentheism posits that the world exists "in" God, who is actively present in the world but not confined to the material universe (Biernacki & Clayton, 2013).

Although UFOs may appear to involve physical objects interacting with their environment through electromagnetic radiation, mechanical and thermal effects, and psychophysiological changes in witnesses, the moral and philosophical implications extend far beyond these physical observations. Tumminia

(2007) astutely observed that, "The believer's mistake is to ascribe meaning and credence to the secondary perception, the mental image created by our brain to account for the stimulus. The skeptic's mistake is to deny the reality of the stimulus altogether, simply because the secondary perception seems absurd. What we take to be reality may, in fact, be a mere appearance, or projection, onto the 'screen' of our four-dimensional space-time world from a much more complex, multidimensional, more fundamental reality" (p. 206). This insight resonates with Plato's allegory of the cave, where sensory reality is revealed as mere shadows on the wall, cast by a higher reality of Ideal Forms beyond the cave. Real progress, therefore, lies not in the extremes of blind belief or outright skepticism, but in navigating the space between these equally rigid attitudes. Spiritist encounters, like UFO phenomena, challenge our conventional understanding of reality, expanding our dualistic and mystic conceptions to encompass a richer, more nuanced view of reality.

4.3 Psychedelic-Occasioned Experience

The term "psychedelic," coined by Humphry Osmond, refers to substances that "manifest the mind," facilitating expanded states of consciousness (Partridge, 2018). Early studies, such as the Good Friday Experiment (Pahnke & Richards, 1966), demonstrated the potential of psychedelics to evoke profound mystical experiences when administered under the proper set and setting. These substances have been described as awakening individuals from an "ontological sleep" (Leary, 1998), suggesting their capacity to reveal deeper layers of reality and self-awareness.

Many commonly used psychedelics occur naturally in the world. For example, mescaline is found in the peyote cactus, psilocybin in magic mushrooms, and N,N-dimethyltryptamine (DMT) in ayahuasca. While LSD is synthesized in laboratories, it shares a key chemical structure with ergot, a psychoactive fungus believed to have played a role in the ancient Greek Eleusinian Mysteries (Muraresku, 2020). The use of these plants has a long history in indigenous cultures worldwide. Examples include the Huichol people's reverence for peyote as a deity, *Hikuri*, and the use of ayahuasca by Amazonian shamans to connect with ancestral spirits. Ethnobotanical studies, such as those by Schultes and colleagues (1992), explore the traditional uses of these plants for spiritual and ritualistic purposes, offering valuable insights into indigenous knowledge and cultural significance of plant-based medicine.

Psychedelic compounds are broadly divided into two major classes. Phenethylamines, such as mescaline, are more associated with dopamine and norepinephrine systems (Shulgin & Shulgin, 1991), while tryptamines, including

DMT and psilocybin, primarily influence serotonin (Shulgin & Shulgin, 1997). Tryptamines are generally more potent than phenethylamines in their psychedelic effect. Recent psychopharmacological studies highlight the effects of classic psychedelics – such as LSD and psilocybin – on neural plasticity through the activation of 5-hydroxytryptamine (serotonin) 2A receptors (5-HT2ARs; Vargas et al., 2023). The REBUS model (relaxed beliefs under psychedelics) posits that psychedelics relax the precision of high-level beliefs, liberating bottom-up information flow, particularly from intrinsic sources like the limbic system (Carhart-Harris et al., 2019). Epidemiological reviews show that classic psychedelics reliably occasion mystical experiences, which are associated with improved psychological outcomes in both healthy volunteers and patient populations (Johnson et al., 2019).

Mystical experiences under the influence of tryptamines often involve contact with dimensions and intelligences beyond the personal or collective human unconscious. These experiences frequently include encounters with organic entelechies – beings that present information not rooted in individual or shared human history, suggesting access to entirely new realms of existence (McKenna, 1991). Laboratory-controlled studies administering DMT have revealed extraordinary personal accounts, detailing encounters with entities that users describe as impossible to dismiss. These reports liken DMT to a reality barometer, allowing users to "change channels" in their perception of reality (Gallimore, 2019; Strassman, 2000). Clinically controlled studies, such as those conducted at the Johns Hopkins Center for Psychedelic and Consciousness Research, have corroborated these observations, highlighting the pivotal role of mystical experiences in the therapeutic efficacy of psychedelics (Griffiths et al., 2006, 2011; Richards, 2015). Similarly, studies supported by the Multidisciplinary Association for Psychedelic Studies have documented the multifaceted impact of psychedelics on human health, creativity, spirituality, and ecological awareness (Doblin & Burge, 2014). Psychedelics are often used for personal spiritual growth. Notable accounts include a twenty-year journey involving seventy-three high-dose LSD sessions (Bache, 2019) and explorations with a variety of psychedelics, including the less common ibogaine, primarily used in Gabon as part of the Bwiti ritual (Pinchbeck, 2002).

Given that individuals often encounter spirits and access nonhuman realms during psychedelic trips, a hypothesis has emerged suggesting that many of the world's religions may have been partially inspired by experiences derived from the use of psychedelic plants (La Barre, 1972). The ingestion of these plants, together with the resulting visions and theriomorphism, has left abundant traces of symbolism in ancient mythology (Ruck, 2018). Wasson (1971) was among the first to examine the use of *soma* in ancient Vedic culture, and later proposed that *kykeon*, the sacramental drink served in the Greek Eleusinian Mysteries, contained a psychoactive ingredient akin to LSD (Wasson et al., 1978). Recent archaeological research has provided additional evidence in support of this hypothesis (Muraresku, 2020). Similar arguments have been advanced regarding the ritual use of *haoma* in Zoroastrian religion (Flattery & Schwartz, 1989), as well as the potential entheogenic roots of ancient Israelite religion, supported by the presence of psychoactive plants in the Sinai Peninsula (Shanon, 2008). These ideas extend further, with some scholars pointing to early Vajrayana Buddhism (Crowley & Shulgin, 2019) and even to the prophetic experiences described in the Hebrew Bible, explored through Strassman's (2014) concept of theoneurology, which posits that divine communication is mediated through the brain.

While these theses are provocative and suggestive, they merely point to the possibility that early religious experiences were facilitated, in part, by the use of psychedelic substances. They will not reduce religion to pharmacology, nor do they explain away the cultural and historical contexts that gave rise to religious traditions (Mosurinjohn & Ascough, 2025). In other words, consciousness-expanding substances are not the "secret key" to unlocking the origins of the world's religions (Greer, 2025). Yet, beyond their potential role in religion, psychedelics may also have played a role in human evolution. McKenna (1992) famously proposed that early human use of psychoactive substances catalyzed brain development and societal advancement. In particular, the consumption of psychedelics such as psilocybin mushrooms may have been pivotal in shaping the evolution of human cognition, language, and spirituality.

The intersection of psychedelics, religion, and mysticism offers profound insights into the nature of transformative experiences and their implications for our understanding of reality. As Latour (2013) emphasizes, religious language functions not to convey factual information but to provoke transformation. Van der Braak (2023) argues that this applies equally to believers who take religious statements as truth claims and secular critics who dismiss them as false. Both are provoked to explore the "more" aspect of reality. Psychedelics, particularly tryptamines like psilocybin and DMT, play a central role in such practices, acting as catalysts for profound shifts in perception and engagement with reality.

However, serious philosophical and theological challenges have been raised regarding the validity of psychedelic-occasioned mysticism. It is crucial to emphasize that the experience itself resides in the individual, not in the substance, and that psychedelics act upon brain neurochemistry merely to occasion, rather than generate, the experience – hence the careful use of the term "occasion." Equally important is the recognition that psychedelic-occasioned experiences are highly variegated, and so too are the psychological assessments that attempt to capture their wide diversity (e.g., Hovmand et al., 2024). While Zaehner (1957) dismissed chemically induced experiences as inauthentic, James's (1902) counterargument against the medical materialists remains no less relevant today: the value of an experience cannot be invalidated simply because its physiological processes are understood. From this perspective, psychedelics may be regarded as tools for transformation, offering experiential access to nonphysical realms that destabilize conventional boundaries of perception and reality. Whether by motivating ritual practices that kindle the perception of the sacred (Luhrmann, 2020) or by fostering encounters with spiritual or nonhuman intelligences, psychedelics open the door to profound experiences that continue to resonate deeply with both religious and mystical traditions.

4.4 Universal Spiritual Principles

Incorporating the experiential knowledge of the spiritual aspects of reality, many theories in the West have emerged to extract and propose universal principles that unify dualistic visions of mysticism into a universal theme. These theories bridge dualistic mysticism with nondualistic and monistic mysticism, as described in previous sections, offering a cohesive framework for understanding the interconnectedness of spiritual and material realities.

Connecting to the experience of spiritist encounters, Anthroposophy posits that humans are spiritual beings living a physical existence, capable of self-development through inner spiritual work. Rudolf Steiner (1913) proposed that the spiritual and material worlds are deeply interconnected and that higher spiritual realities can be accessed through disciplined practices such as meditation, ethical self-discipline, and imagination. Anthroposophy seeks to bridge the gap between natural science and spiritual science, offering a holistic view of human existence and evolution as a path to higher consciousness.

A more ancient and foundational theory is Hermeticism, which traces its origins to Late Antiquity and is attributed to the mythical figure Hermes Trismegistus. Hermeticism proposes universal principles that explain the nature of reality and guide spiritual understanding. These principles include the idea that the universe is a mental construct, the correspondence between heaven and earth encapsulated in the phrase "as above, so below," the notion that everything is in constant vibration, the cyclical nature of life, and the coexistence of masculine and feminine aspects in all creation (Hall, 2007). Reinterpreted in modern times, Hermetic philosophy combines Greek rationality with Egyptian mythology, evolving into a mystical method that guides experiential practices aimed at achieving direct spiritual knowledge (Hanegraaff, 2022). Practitioners of Hermeticism engage in spiritual exercises such as luminous visions and exorcism to perceive reality beyond appearances. Hermeticism also celebrates embodiment as a divine gift, enabling humans to cocreate with nature and participate in the unfolding of the cosmos.

Building on these ideas, Theosophy emerged as a modern esoteric movement that synthesizes Hermeticism with Eastern spirituality and occult traditions. While earlier figures like Emanuel Swedenborg laid the groundwork with his mystical visions of heaven and hell, the modern expression of Theosophy began with Helena Blavatsky, who cofounded the Theosophical Society in 1875. Blavatsky's (1895) work integrated Eastern mysticism with Western esoteric thought, focusing on spiritual evolution and the idea of a universal wisdom underlying all religions. Theosophy emphasizes the active and creative imagination as a key faculty that bridges material and spiritual realities. Through symbols, rituals, and mediating entities, individuals can access higher levels of existence and achieve spiritual transformation (Faivre, 2000). Esotericism serves as an umbrella term that encompasses Hermeticism, Theosophy, and other occult traditions. Western esotericism is characterized by several key themes: symbolic connections between all parts of the universe, viewing the cosmos as alive and spiritually interconnected, focusing on personal transformation through esoteric knowledge, seeking commonalities across spiritual traditions, and stressing the passage of knowledge through initiation from master to disciple (Faivre & Needleman, 1992).

In addition to these abstract philosophical ideas, some theories have sought to express universal principles in more concrete terms. For example, Karl von Reichenbach (1850) proposed the concept of a universal life energy, which he called the "Odic force." This subtle energy, related to magnetism and electricity, was believed to permeate all living and nonliving matter. Reichenbach suggested that the Odic force could explain phenomena such as hypnotism and other sensory experiences. Although the theory emphasizes the material aspects of this force – such as its radiation from substances like magnets and crystals – it most importantly implies a universal, nonphysical medium underlying physical phenomena.

Resonating with the themes of nondualistic mysticism discussed in comparative religious perspectives, certain universal mental constructs were proposed prior to the development of comparative frameworks. One such concept is "elementary ideas" (*Elementargedanken*), introduced by Adolf Bastian (1895). Bastian's theory served as a precursor to Carl Jung's idea of the collective unconscious and contributed to the field of comparative mythology. According to Bastian, elementary ideas are universal, transcultural, and transhistorical mental constructs shared by all humans due to the psychic unity of mankind. These ideas represent the fundamental building blocks of human thought, akin to cells in biology, and are expressed differently across cultures as folk ideas (*Völkergedanken*).

All these attempts to uncover universal spiritual principles culminate in a transition from "a religion of all religions" to "a religion of no-religion." Frederic Spiegelberg (1948) argued for a process of deconstructing religions, beginning with monotheism, which denies the gods of other traditions, progressing to pantheism, which sees God as living in everything and everywhere – and thus nowhere – and culminating in an abstract gnostic or mystical insight. In this final stage, gods are understood as manifestations of the human spirit, and the division between self and cosmos dissolves. Ultimately, the concept of "no-religion" serves as a form of spirituality that transcends binary visions of spiritual worlds and traditional religious structures, bringing us full circle to monistic mysticism.

5 Pluralistic Mysticism

The fourth layer is pluralistic mysticism, one that extends beyond the simple dichotomy of human and nonhuman realms to embrace the coexistence of multiple potentials of reality and the manifold aspects of the self. Reality may be conceived as physical, nonphysical, or physical yet susceptible to influence by mental capacities. Likewise, the self may be experienced as both rooted in the body and felt as essentially mental. This form of mysticism transcends fixed boundaries, diversifying realities into infinite possibilities and ultimately transforming the self by unveiling its boundless potential. Within such an expanded framework, all conceivable forms of mysticism become possible. It may encompass dualistic mysticism, in which higher or lower spiritual beings inhabit realities parallel to human existence; nondualistic mysticism, which gestures toward idealized versions of human reality; and monistic mysticism, which discloses universal principles uniting all realities and all selves into a single whole.

This section begins with nonphysicalism, which entertains the possible existence of a nonmaterial counterpart to physical reality and highlights the foundational character of the mind as unbounded by material constraints. From this foundation, the discussion turns to parapsychological phenomena that challenge conventional physical explanations, raising the possibility that mental capacities may affect physical realities. It then moves to embodied spirituality, which illustrates the interwoven nature of physical and nonphysical aspects of the self that give rise to boundless human potential, showing even the spiritual to be capable of manifestation in somatic forms. Finally, the section culminates in a discussion of consciousness, emphasizing its capacity to transcend and survive the body. Within this perspective, the brain functions not as the source of consciousness but as its receiver. Reality, accordingly, is not singular or unified but comprised of multiple potentials, each accessible through distinct human faculties. This plurality suggests infinite possibilities, with our commonly perceived physical reality existing as only one among many potential realities. The unification of these diverse elements becomes not merely an abstract metaphysical claim but a deeply personal mission to be undertaken and fulfilled within this lifetime.

5.1 Nonphysicalism

With reality being commonly perceived as rooted in materialist components, the possibility of nonphysical realities has long been marginalized under the dominance of the physicalist paradigm. This paradigm displays a distinct bias, neglecting the mental insights manifest in the experiences of mystics, shamans, and psychics. Recognizing this limitation, the first observation is that the mind is more than merely physical. Recent research has marked a paradigm shift toward nonphysicalism, with a growing body of edited volumes contending that consciousness cannot be reduced to physical brain processes alone. Anomalous data – such as near-death experiences, clairvoyance, and other psychic phenomena – suggest that consciousness may, at least under certain conditions, operate independently of the brain (Kelly et al., 2007). Building upon such findings, scholars have proposed a new metaphysical framework to explain how reality must be structured in order to accommodate phenomena that transcend physicalist assumptions (Kelly et al., 2015). Ultimately, the integration of extraordinary experiences into a broader vision of reality highlights the possibility that human beings embody spiritual dimensions and capacities that remain largely untapped (Kelly & Marshall, 2021).

Attempts to reconcile known physics with the nonphysical world have either sought to extend existing scientific paradigms or to develop a quasi-scientific language for describing the nonphysical. Quantum mechanics has frequently been invoked as a conceptual bridge between physics and mysticism, though many early writings arguably lean more toward mysticism than rigorous science (Capra, 1975). Perhaps the most well-known attempt is the Pauli–Jung conjecture, which proposes a unified framework bridging mind and matter through a psychophysically neutral reality. This theory posits that mental and physical phenomena are dual aspects of an underlying, indivisible reality, interwoven through archetypal patterns and meaningful correlations such as synchronicity

(Atmanspacher & Fuchs, 2014). Theories that are derived from eastern philosophy similarly posit the existence of a corresponding spiritual space mirroring the physical world (Li, 2018).

Conceptualizing reality and consciousness as dynamic systems rather than discrete states has led to diverse models. Bohm's (1980) theory of holomovement posits that reality is an undivided whole, in which the implicate order (a hidden, interconnected reality) unfolds into the explicate order (the observable world), with all elements dynamically interconnected. In a holographic system, each part contains information about the whole, so even if sections are damaged or removed, the overall pattern or information can still be reconstructed from the remaining parts. The holographic theory of brain function, therefore, suggests that memories and perceptions are distributed across neural networks rather than localized in specific structures (Pribram, 1971). Consciousness may therefore converge into a vast informational pool. Bateson (1979) emphasizes "the pattern that connects" – a unifying principle linking life, evolution, and learning – arguing that cognition is not confined to human consciousness but embedded within the broader natural world, governed by patterns, feedback loops, and relationships. Similarly, Laszlo (2004) proposes the existence of the "Akashic Field," a nonmaterial informational substrate underlying all of reality, containing the imprints of past, present, and future events. The theory of morphogenetic fields suggests that biological and behavioral patterns emerge from collective memory, with organisms inheriting learned traits through morphic resonance rather than genetic transmission (Sheldrake, 1981).

Reality has also been construed as existing in nonphysical, energetic forms. Naranjo (2006) contends that the experience of energetic states is not confined to specific cultures but represents a universally accessible potential, deeply embedded in human physiology as a pathway to enlightenment. One might perceive "an ever-shifting tonus dance that takes place in our muscle system in the situation of ego dissolution;" yet anatomically, this may be understood as "coordinated volleys of nerve impulses that follow preestablished patterns" (pp. 57–58). The consistency of perception in the waking world, contrasted with its variability in dreams, raises the question of distinguishing mental projection from true reality. One method is through the observation of energy: beings that glow with energy are more real, whereas projections lack this vitality (Castaneda, 1993).

Throughout history, numerous methods for observing the nonphysical have been developed, many incorporated within religious traditions. In Confucianism and Traditional Chinese Medicine, the technique of *neizheng* ("internal observation") enables perception through spiritual sight. Under such observation, the nonexistence comes into existence for the internal observer;

without such observation, it remains nonexistent. In this view, existence and nonexistence in Chinese philosophy are differentiated solely by observational methodology. Both exist but require different methods to be seen (Anonymous, 2009). Beyond observation, consciousness may also exert influence over the quantum world, producing observable effects (Mensky, 2010). Quantum interactive dualism posits that the mind affects physical reality by collapsing quantum wave functions, bridging the gap between mental intention and physical manifestation (Stapp, 2007).

Expanding beyond physicalist assumptions offers a conceptual liberation from rigid, singular reality, allowing for models that embrace multiple ontological existences. However, due caution is warranted in the construction of any universal theory. Human development has been theorized to progress through successive stages – gross (focused on nature), subtle (experiencing deity), causal/witness (formless), and nondual – as well as through archaic, magical, mythic, rational, pluralistic, integral, and super-integral stages (Wilber, 2017). Each stage implies a distinct ontological status, mapped according to its "kosmic address" within specific existential workspaces. To access these realities, one needs only to establish contact with the corresponding workspaces.

5.2 Parapsychological Phenomena

Not only could realities exist in nonphysical forms, but physical realities themselves may also be impacted by mental capacities. The family of phenomena most relevant to this hypothesis is parapsychology. As an umbrella term, parapsychology encompasses a range of interrelated concepts that describe experiences or events transcending ordinary sensory perception and the boundaries of conventional physics. This includes both psychic and paranormal phenomena. Psychic phenomena involve extrasensory perception and psychokinesis – collectively termed *psi* – as well as events suggesting the existence of spirit independent of the body, such as near-death experiences (Owens et al., 1990; Zaleski, 1987). Paranormal phenomena, in turn, refer to occurrences that defy conventional scientific explanation or natural laws, including ghost sightings, Kirlian auras, and psychic healing. Kripal (2010) distinguishes the two by noting that in psychic vision, the transcendent moves from the religious register into a scientific one, whereas in paranormal events, the transcendent departs from both religious and scientific registers altogether, entering a still undefined realm – what he terms an "impossible" order of things (p. 72). Related concepts include the *supernormal* and the *supernatural*, both pointing to phenomena beyond ordinary experience – suggesting either a higher evolutionary stage or transcendental laws, though not necessarily outside of nature itself.

It must be noted at the outset that many so-called supernatural and paranormal phenomena have been debunked and deemed inexplicable within the framework of physics. No existing scientific consensus has been reached on the veridicality of most such claims. Perhaps precisely because of their controversial character, the most rigorous studies and critiques of paranormal claims have been undertaken by leading physical scientists (Abell & Singer, 1981). The general consensus is that psychic experiences – including telepathy, precognition, psychokinesis, and apparitions – are more prevalent than commonly assumed, yet do not all require supernatural explanations (Henry, 2004). Many can be more coherently interpreted through psychological, cultural, or neurological frameworks (Taylor, 1980). The point, however, is not to prove whether any of these phenomena are real, but rather to reflect on the implications of what it would mean if they were real. In particular, realities cannot be reduced to human perception alone; under different modes of perception, realities may appear in radically different forms.

Recent perspectives increasingly conceptualize parapsychology as a natural extension of scientific inquiry, governed by principles that may apply simultaneously to physical and transcendental domains (Radin, 2013), and closely tied to the neurobiological foundations of human cognition (Craffert et al., 2019). The significance of parapsychology lies in its potential to illuminate hidden interconnections that bind the universe together, offering a cornerstone for the construction of new metaphysical frameworks in science (Kelly et al., 2015). Rather than dismissing such occurrences as anomalous violations of natural law, they may point toward the existence of higher evolutionary stages or laws that transcend ordinary human experience (Fort, 1932). Crucially, while contemporary science often restricts itself to mechanistic descriptions, psi phenomena appear fundamentally concerned with questions of meaning and purpose (Radin, 1997).

Psychological realities are likely not merely a complement to physical realities, but may in fact constitute the majority, with physical reality representing only a minority. It is as though the universe is composed largely of dark energy, with observable matter remaining scarce. James (1902) long argued that our normal waking consciousness is only one particular mode of awareness among many. Alternative states – including hypnagogic states (between waking and sleeping), dreams, meditative absorption, hypnosis, psychosis, and psychedelic experience – each manifest distinct domains of applicability and adaptation. Jung (1953) further emphasized the primacy of psychic reality, insisting that subjective experience is the only immediately verifiable category of existence: "Psychic existence is the only category of existence of which we have immediate knowledge, since nothing can be known unless it first appears as a psychic image. Only psychic existence is immediately verifiable. To the extent that the world does not assume the form of a psychic image, it is virtually nonexistent" (p. 769).

Parapsychological phenomena also share deep resonances with dualistic and nondualistic forms of mysticism. The long-standing notion of magic has often been divided into three primary types (Radin, 2018). *Divination* involves gaining insight or knowledge across time and space through non-ordinary means, such as tarot reading, astrology, and other techniques for perceiving hidden information. *Force of Will* refers to the ability to influence reality through intention, encompassing psychokinesis and other mind-over-matter effects where focused consciousness shapes the external world. *Theurgy* entails interaction with spiritual entities or higher intelligences, often through ceremonial practices designed to evoke guidance or assistance. These categories not only incorporate psychical and paranormal capacities but also resonate with spiritist techniques and the invocation of higher beings characteristic of both dualistic and nondualistic mysticism.

Parapsychological phenomena and monistic mysticism may share a common origin in practices of deep meditative concentration and one-pointed attention. Such states can be cultivated actively – through disciplined quieting of the mind – or passively, by allowing subconscious imagery to arise. Mystics are frequently described not only as exemplars of extraordinary spiritual purity and direct communion with the divine, but also as figures possessing remarkable abilities: levitation, telepathic perception, aura vision, journeys into spirit worlds, clairvoyant witnessing of distant events, psychokinetic manipulation of objects, and spiritual healing (Hollenback, 1996). Once again, a common thread emerges, linking monistic mysticism, parapsychology, and the broader fabric of human experience – suggesting dimensions of reality irreducible to physicalist reductionism.

5.3 Embodied Spirituality

Not unlike the multiple possibilities inherent in the forms of existence of reality, the self, too, can exist in both physical and nonphysical forms. While the spiritual aspect of one's self – such as the soul – is often experienced as a psychological entity, it may in fact be capable of manifestation in material forms. The case that best illustrates the intertwining of the physical and nonphysical self is that of embodied spirituality. A longstanding notion asserts that the body itself serves as a source of spiritual knowledge: "The human body is a microcosm that reflects and contains the entire macrocosm; if one could thoroughly explore one's own body and psyche, this would bring the knowledge of all the phenomenal worlds" (Grof, 1998, p. 110). In this sense, body and spirit need not be construed as distinct or opposing entities; rather, they are different aspects along the continuum of human experience (Johnson, 1994). Accordingly, the future of human potential may be envisioned in terms of a soul-body integralism, which proposes that human development entails the integration of both physical and spiritual evolution, with consciousness not separate from the body but unfolding through embodied experiences, mystical practices, and transformative states (Murphy, 1992).

The participatory model of the human position in the cosmos further suggests that an inward truth within human beings links the self to the larger cosmological order, where the inner world possesses a reality deeper than its outer reflection (Flood, 2013). Within this framework, the cosmos is conceived as containing a hierarchy of levels that are mapped onto the vertical structure of the human body, and this inner truth is accessed through visualization and ritual practices that connect the person to the cosmos. The sacrality of human life, therefore, lies not in autonomous individualism but in participation in the order of being. The habits cultivated through ritual and meditation become formative practices that shape a way of life, aligning one's being with forms and forces greater than the self. Related views hold that the premodern self possessed porous boundaries through which cosmological forces – such as spirits – could permeate it, in contrast to the buffered self of modernity, which perceives the world in horizontal terms, lacking vertical or transcendent dimensions (Taylor, 2007).

However, mysticism that involves sensory content has often been valued less than monistic mysticism devoid of form. This position is exemplified by a fourteenth-century Augustinian mystic: "Visions of revelations by spirits, whether seen in bodily form or in the imagination, and whether in sleeping or waking, do not constitute true contemplation. This applies equally to any other sensible experiences of seemingly spiritual origin, whether of sound, taste, smell, or of warmth felt like a glowing fire in the breast or in other parts of the body – anything, indeed, that can be experienced by the physical senses" (Hilton, 1990, pp. 14–15). A similar distinction between lower (sensate) and higher (transcendent) contemplative states appears in the Yogasutra texts, which assert that conscious concentration is only a preliminary step to deeper states of meditation that transcend object-consciousness (Woods, 1914).

Central to the claim of embodied spirituality is the presence of supernormal bodily abilities. In the *Yogasutra*, Book 4, Patanjali describes how *siddhis* (perfections) and *vibhutis* (powers) can be attained through birth, drugs, mantras, asceticism, and concentration (Woods, 1914). In Buddhism, as illustrated in the *Abhidharmakosa*, the Buddha did not prohibit the attainment of these powers (*abhijna* or *rddhi*) but discouraged their exhibition to laypersons

(Eliade, 1958). A further example is the experience, by some, an innate power within the human body that can be awakened. One such power is Kundalini, a dormant spiritual force coiled at the base of the spine, which, when activated, ascends through the body, leading to heightened consciousness, mystical visions, and psychic abilities (Krishna, 1971). Vivekananda (2016) described the principles of Kundalini as involving two nerve currents, *Pingala* and *Ida*, running along the spinal column, with a hollow canal called *Sushumna* at the center. At the lower end of this canal is what Yogis term the "Lotus of the Kundalini," a coiled energy. When awakened, Kundalini rises step by step, opening different layers of the mind, unveiling visions and extraordinary abilities. Upon reaching the brain, the Yogi attains complete detachment from body and mind, experiencing ultimate spiritual liberation. A similar view of the body appears in Daoist traditions, where the *jing* and *luo* meridian systems circulate *qi*, sustaining spiritual and physical vitality (Scheid, 2007).

Neuroscience has identified brain circuitries fundamental to primary emotional experiences, such as PLAY and SEEKING, which are directly relevant to spiritual experiences (Panksepp & Biven, 2012). The PLAY system, rooted in subcortical brain regions and modulated by neurochemicals like dopamine and opioids, fosters social joy and bonding. The SEEKING system, centered on the mesolimbic dopamine system, drives exploration, goal-directed behavior, and reward anticipation. Neuroimaging findings suggest that religious and spiritual experiences also intersect with human sexuality, as both activate the brain's reward circuits, particularly the *nucleus accumbens*, which plays a central role in processing pleasure and reward (Newberg, 2024). Moreover, certain mystical experiences can be induced through direct brain stimulation (Blanke et al., 2002).

While physiological data support the embodiment of mysticism, a crucial caveat remains: electrochemical signals in the brain are not identical to subjective feelings, beliefs, and experiences. Observable phenomena do not map systematically or one-to-one onto conscious experiences. In other words, the brain is not *designed* for spirituality alone; rather, mystical experience utilizes the same neural circuits as more mundane experiences without diminishing its significance. Furthermore, conditions do not equate to causes – being in the same physiological state does not necessarily produce the same experience. Spontaneity remains a defining characteristic of mysticism (Jones, 1986).

5.4 Consciousness

The ultimate challenge to the rigid bifurcation that posits reality as only physical and spirituality as only nonphysical emerges most clearly in the so-called "hard problem of consciousness." This enduring problem draws both the material brain and the nonmaterial dimensions of consciousness into the perception of reality: neither can the brain be said to exclusively produce consciousness, nor can consciousness be said to merely conjure the brain; rather, what is at stake is the intricate, reciprocal relationship between the two (Chalmers, 1996). A longstanding hypothesis, known as the Myers–James Transmission thesis, proposes that the brain functions less as a generator and more as a receiver, with consciousness transmitting through it (James, 1899; Myers, 1903). From this perspective, consciousness preexists the brain, which serves primarily to modulate it into perceptible forms. This view resonates with the filter thesis (Bergson, 1988) and with interpretations of psychedelic states as conditions in which the brain's filtering mechanism is suspended or loosened, thereby allowing broader ranges of consciousness to become manifest (Grof, 1998). Such ideas collectively envision the physical world as an interconnected, dynamic continuum of becoming, in which innumerable vibrations interweave in unbroken continuity, propagating through existence like ripples across an immense body. Within this framework, the material universe – understood as the totality of images – is itself a form of consciousness. The brain, then, is not a productive organ but a receptive one, and reality at its core is nothing less than consciousness.

The case of reincarnation provides a compelling illustration of consciousness transcending the brain, suggesting that it is received and further developed into a new individual. Among the most prominent figures in this area, Ian Stevenson (1974) conducted extensive research documenting cases that strongly support reincarnation. His work presented detailed case studies from various cultures, highlighting recurring patterns such as children recalling past-life identities, describing previous experiences, and exhibiting behaviors or phobias linked to their alleged past deaths. Further corroborating evidence includes physical phenomena such as birthmarks and defects corresponding to fatal wounds in a previous life (Stevenson, 2001). The question raised by reincarnation, however, is nuanced: what, precisely, is reincarnated? Is it the superessential and indivisible divine element, or the surviving personality, an aggregation of emotions, mind, and personal memories? Or is it both? Theosophists emphasize the former, while Stevenson's work lends support to the latter. "The Pilgrim is the only immortal and eternal principle in us, being an indivisible part of the integral whole – the Universal Spirit – from which it emanates, and into which it is absorbed at the end of the cycle" (Blavatsky, 1895, p. 16).

Successors in this field have furthered investigations into "life before life" (Tucker, 2005) and "life after life" (Moody, 1975), as well as the phenomenon of out-of-body experiences (OBEs; Buhlman, 1996). OBEs have been understood not merely as hallucinations but as transformative journeys revealing the existence of a "Second Body" – a nonphysical aspect of the self capable of traversing dimensions beyond material reality. Counterarguments exist, particularly the view that OBEs are not evidence of the soul departing the body but rather psychological and neurological constructs (Blackmore, 1982). According to this perspective, OBEs occur when the brain generates an alternative model of reality, shifting perspective to a bird's-eye view through memory and imagination. However, at the psychological level, the experience of pluralistic forms of the self – ranging from the embodied individual to the disembodied spirit – is undeniable to those who undergo it.

A further dimension of consciousness research concerns its evolution and role in shaping human identity. The consciousness we recognize today is a relatively recent development in human history. Before its emergence, human cognition functioned within a "bicameral" framework, wherein the brain's hemispheres operated semi-independently. The left hemisphere (more associated with language and logic) "spoke" to the right hemisphere (more responsible for action and intuition), with these communications often perceived as external voices or divine commands. Jaynes (1976) argued that the collapse of this system led to self-awareness and introspection, thus birthing modern consciousness. Expanding on this idea, McGilchrist (2019) proposed that while the brain's hemispheres collaborate on various cognitive tasks, they allocate attention in markedly different ways: the left hemisphere privileges analytical detail and control, whereas the right hemisphere emphasizes holistic perception, intuition, and subjective experience. Continuing this line of thought, Neumann (1954), drawing from Jungian theory, posited that consciousness arises through the dialectical interplay between the unconscious and conscious mind, with myths and symbols serving as reflective expressions of this developmental process. He further suggested that early human consciousness was dominated by matriarchal symbolism – associated with fertility and nature – before transitioning to patriarchal structures that prioritized ego-consciousness and rationality.

These extended theoretical models of consciousness and reality offer valuable insights into spiritual development and healing. Grof (2019) proposed a pluralistic mysticism framework encompassing perinatal experiences, archetypal encounters, past-life recollections, the collective unconscious, and cosmic consciousness. His research into mystical consciousness – whether induced by psychedelics or accessed through holotropic breathwork – suggests an inner healing intelligence that enables individuals to navigate and integrate the multiplicities of personal experience. At a cultural level, Metzner (2022) identified recurrent motifs and archetypes in transformative experiences, including metaphors such as the "journey," "death and rebirth," and the "remembering" of the self, all of which symbolize the reintegration of fragmented aspects of consciousness. This pluralistic mysticism, expressed through both physical and nonphysical existence as well as various states of consciousness, ultimately converges in the lifelong process of self-discovery and integration – a spiritual task each individual is called to fulfill in this lifetime.

6 Philosophical Reflections

In this Element, mysticism is characterized as a family of extraordinary experiences that *transcend perceived reality and transform the individual*. This definition gives rise to a layered hierarchy model of mysticism, structured across four interconnected yet distinct layers. These layers are ordered based on multiple criteria. In terms of transformed selfhood, the progression moves from a state of no-self (monistic), to a self subsumed into an ideal (nondualistic), followed by a dichotomy between self and nonhuman realms (dualistic), and finally, to a recognition of multiple potentials within the self (pluralistic). A similar ordering applies to the status of perceived reality, ranging from an all-encompassing unity to the recognition of multiple realities. This hierarchy also extends to the role of the body in mystical experiences: in monistic mysticism, the body is formless; in nondualistic mysticism, it may be viewed as an impediment to the soul's liberation; in dualistic mysticism, spiritual teachings are often channeled through the body; and in pluralistic mysticism, the body is seen as essential for realizing spiritual potential. This framework also reflects a continuum from the least culturally bound – a contentless monistic unity – to the most attuned to situational and cultural contexts in pluralistic realities.

This system, capturing a broad spectrum of transcendence and transformation, argues that at the level of experience, most extraordinary experiences share common psychological reflections. The aim is neither to propose yet another model of mysticism nor to conflate narrowly defined monistic mysticism with other affiliated experiences. Rather, this approach aligns with Staal's (1975) fundamental recommendation that the study of mysticism should shift its focus away from theoretical superstructures and return to experiences themselves. Accordingly, this Element attempts to refocus on the experiential dimension, identifying a common thread that weaves through these extraordinary human experiences. The layered hierarchy model, as demonstrated in Figure 2 and Table 1, does not exhaust all possible modes of existence, and there are innumerable mystical experiences that may fit within this definition while not being fully described by the four layers. As demonstrated, these layers are not rigidly defined or isolated; rather, experiences within one layer often flow into those of another, with unitive vision emerging as a commonality across all layers of mysticism. At the most fundamental level, the subject of awareness, the act of being aware, and the object of awareness are not separate but constitute the experience itself. They *are* the experience.

The final section brings all these elements together. First, it reinforces an openness to experiences of transcendent realities, guided by the humility of ontological agnosticism. Second, it affirms that all transcendent realities, while supernormal, remain within natural confines – not contravening known natural laws but rather operating at a level that overrides them. Third, it asserts that transcended realities necessitate a transformed self to be fully experienced, leading to a discussion on how mystical lessons should be integrated into daily life. Finally, it explores the moral implications of mysticism, emphasizing that the transformed self does not remain in an ecstatic realm but returns to live life to its fullest. The ultimate revelation is that everything lies in the here and now – that the meaning of life is not a distant pursuit but an experience of being fully alive. The circle is complete, or in Chan Buddhist terms, the nature of reality is true emptiness, yet wondrous existence.

6.1 Transcendent Realities

The transcendent realities that emerge in mystical visions occupy a unique category that transcends the binary of real and unreal. The term *imaginal*, coined by Henry Corbin (1977), aptly situates the mystical dimension beyond both the physical and the imaginary, the latter typically referring to what is not real. The imaginal constitutes a psychical mode of cognition that, under the right circumstances and with proper training, mediates communication between the divine order and the human mind through coded symbols, visionary or dream phenomena, mythical material, and paradoxical doctrines of profound depth. Numerous cosmological models integrate both the observable physical universe and potential, unobserved spiritual realms. Among these, hyperdimensional models resonate with "esoteric accounts of extraspatial worlds in which our familiar existence is embedded, and from which phantom figures, luminosities, odors of sanctity, and other extrasomatic phenomena materialize, and through which highly developed spirit-bodies move" (Murphy, 1992, pp. 217–218).

An inherent hierarchy may structure these different realities. In such models, each level encompasses and transcends the ones below it while being encompassed by those above. The quantum physical realm, for example, does not stand parallel to the realm of higher consciousness (Wilber, 2017). Monistic mysticism is often situated at the highest level, following the Platonic *great chain of being*, where mystical unity surpasses other religious experiences (Smith, 1976). This prioritization recurs across traditions: "We have the West Asian God beyond God, the South Asian nirguna Brahman beyond saguna Brahman, and the East Asian

Dao that cannot be described beyond proximate realities" (Wildman, 2010, p. 295). However, the layered hierarchy proposed in this Element does not necessarily endorse such hierarchical relationships among various types and levels of dependent experiences. Instead, it aligns more closely with a "sparse ontology," positing only a fundamental ontological contrast between ultimate reality and dependent reality, without hierarchical stratification or ethical consequences (Wildman, 2010). In a sparse ontology, different types and levels of being serve as symbolic engagements with ultimate reality, emerging within each dependent reality as individuals strive to make sense of their world.

In line with this position, the psychology of mysticism underscores two key principles. The first is ontological agnosticism, which maintains a neutral stance on the metaphysical status of reality (e.g., whether ultimate reality exists). Mysticism is thus characterized as the transcendence of perceived reality – where *perceived* is critical, as we make no claims regarding whether the various realities experienced are real or imagined. The second is phenomenological realism, which asserts that immediate experience can provide genuine insight into objective reality (e.g., how ultimate reality manifests). In other words, experience takes precedence. While this philosophical stance is conceptually rich, it presents a practical challenge: how can one remain agnostic about what lies beyond experience while simultaneously affirming that the world is not merely a mental construct?

The recent ontological turn in cultural anthropology offers a response to this dilemma. In the study of mysticism, the previous epistemological concern – how one perceives reality – shifts toward the ontological question of *what there is to perceive* (Ferrer & Sherman, 2008; Holbraad & Pedersen, 2017). This turn is not merely a shift in perspective, shaped by social and cultural presuppositions, but a deeper transformation in how different aspects of reality are perceived. This move echoes Latour's (1993) critique of modernity, which argues that the distinctions between transcendence and immanence, between external objects and internal subjective experience, and between human and nonhuman worlds are not fundamental truths but constructs of modernity. The previous paradigm of multiculturalism emphasized a single nature with multiple cultures, focusing on epistemological complexity (Bellah, 2011). A step forward is *multinaturalism*, which posits a unity of spirit and a diversity of bodies. In this framework, every being – human or nonhuman – functions as a potential center of intentionality, capable of perceiving the world according to its own nature and potentialities (Viveiros de Castro, 2014). Echoing Latour's critique of modernity and the proposal for multinaturalism, the model of mysticism presented here seeks to dissolve rigid boundaries and illuminate the vast spectrum of potential experiences.

6.2 Super but Natural

Although mysticism opens pathways to realities vastly different from the mundane, it is crucial to recognize that these seemingly supernormal phenomena do not contravene natural laws but rather override them (Myers, 1903). Murphy (1992) later termed these experiences *metanormal* capacities. Both Myers and Murphy insisted on naturalizing the supernatural, collapsing any rigid boundaries between the sacred and the profane. There is no inherent conflict between transcendence and knowledge; insight can emerge both from external observation – such as through scientific tools, and from gnosis, intuition, or direct introspective observation within the psyche. Apparitions, for instance – whether visions of ghosts or of the Virgin Mary, as in Lourdes – may arise from below the threshold of one's own psyche. A living or deceased psyche's subliminal substance can persist in some space and interact with another human psyche, providing a psychological framework for mystical encounters. The psychology of mysticism incorporates two perspectives that shape how reality and the nature of being are understood and perceived. These perspectives can be categorized as: (1) the empirical, material, quantitative, rational, and analytical, and (2) the nonempirical, nonmaterial, qualitative, suprarational, and synthetic (Quinn, 1997). Rather than standing in opposition, these two dimensions of existence complement one another, each offering its own lens for interpreting mystical phenomena.

This discussion is further enriched by the ontological debate between *ground of being* mysticism – a form of essentialism that assumes some ultimate reality upon which all existence is based – and a *network view* of mysticism. The latter, influenced by Latour's principle of irreduction – "Nothing can be reduced to anything else, nothing can be deduced from anything else, everything may be allied to everything else" (Latour, 1988, p. 163) – offers a compelling alternative to essentialist models. Here, interconnectedness and irreducibility take precedence over fixed hierarchies, paralleling the Hindu philosophical distinction between the knowledge to be established (*sadhya*) and the already established (*siddha*). Advaita Vedanta and Buddhism transcend this dichotomy entirely, presenting an absolute framework that integrates both being and becoming.

This interplay between being and becoming manifests across mystical traditions as the tension between eternal, unrevealed truth and that which is continually verified by human experience. Perhaps its explicit goal is to make mysticism not only intelligible but also applicable to the mundane world – a pragmatism that resonates deeply with Daoism. In the *Daode jing* 42, this principle unfolds rapidly from an abstract principle to everything in the visible world: "Dao begets one, one begets two, two begets three, three begets the myriad things." Just as *Halakhah* in Judaism and *Dao* in Daoism serve as both cosmic principles and pragmatic ethics, these frameworks underscore the relevance of mystical insights to embodied life.

This brings us full circle, connecting monistic mysticism to a broader pluralistic framework. The layered hierarchy model does not claim an ultimate primacy but instead establishes dimensions along which mystical variations can be described and expressed. At the heart of mystical experience lies an ineffable *something* sensed in the depths of nature – neither a concrete being nor pure nonexistence. Plotinus (1956) articulates this paradox, conceiving the One as a singular nothingness from which all existence emerges: "It is precisely because there is nothing within the One that all things are from it" (V.1.1). In this way, mysticism balances perennial wisdom with relativism, embracing the plurality of human cultural practices while resisting forms of relativism that fail to distinguish between traditions that nurture and those that harm embodied existence (Kripal, 2008).

6.3 Transformed Self

Transcendent reality requires a transformed self to grasp it (Wittmann, 2018). The hierarchy of realities is also reflected in how these realities are received by the perceiver. Myers (1903) delineates three stages of subliminal life in humanity, each revealing different layers of mysticism: the inspiration of dream, genius, and psychosis, in which the subliminal doors are opened by sleep, skill, or psychological disintegration; the psychic phenomena of telepathic communication with a departed or still-living mind, bearing witness to the supernormal potentials inherent in all; and the complete takeover of the conscious self in trance, possession, and ecstasy.

Across these different states of transformation, the primary challenge lies in integrating the insights gained from these altered states into ordinary consciousness. A common difficulty arises when individuals engaged in mystical practices aimed at personal growth isolate these experiences from the rest of their lives. Yet, true growth must occur within everyday existence, just as profound revelations gained from meditative practice must be studied in relation to ordinary living (Maupin, 1972). Spiritual practices should not aim to eliminate the everyday self – often judged as an impostor – but rather to harmonize this relatively ignorant and isolated self with the underlying reality, achieving a conscious integration (Marshall, 2019).

The real learning often unfolds long after the mystical experience itself. In the psychedelic context, for instance, one is encouraged to sit with the experience, allowing it to unfold over time rather than expecting instant transformation.

Psychedelic effects are a delicate interplay of psychological set and setting, where the substance itself serves merely as a trigger or facilitating agent. Far from being an effortless path to growth, many report that the subjective labor experienced during a psychedelic session can be as arduous and exhausting as several years of ordinary life. However, the most challenging work comes afterward, in the process of integrating newfound insights into daily existence (Pahnke & Richards, 1966).

Another dimension of this process involves the participation of others. Mystics may initiate new knowledge, but they rely on social transmission to impart these insights to the wider community. This is evident in classical Chinese medicine, a practice built upon the transmission of skills and expertise from master to novice. As novices mature into masters themselves, they not only transform their own identities but also shape the evolving definition of the practice's goals and values. To accomplish this, human beings need narratives – stories that define who they are, what they do, and why they do it. Traditions provide these narratives, offering frameworks for identifying problems, developing methods of resolution, and constructing institutions that facilitate cooperative action (Scheid, 2007). Mysticism, over time, solidifies into institutions (Hood & Chen, 2012). Troeltsch (1931) identified a progression in religious movements: a mystically oriented *cult* centered on a divine element within the individual evolves into a socially marginalized *sect* organized around a charismatic leader, which, in turn, matures into an established *church* that no longer requires demonstrations of faith but instead maintains the religious status quo.

In a religious setting, the ultimate aim is not mystical experience itself, but the religious life (Smith, 2000). Clark (1958) defines religion as the individual's inner experience of sensing a "Beyond," particularly as evidenced by the impact of this experience on behavior – when one actively seeks to harmonize life with that Beyond. Jewish tradition, for instance, insists on linking profound inner experiences with a communicable and verifiable word, transforming received revelation into externally applicable law (Weiner, 1969). In short, what ultimately matters is not what one feels, but how one acts in the world.

Yet, mystical experience is often hard to cultivate and may have limited pragmatic effects on an individual's daily life. Unlike visions or shamanic journeys, which can be cultivated through deliberate practice, the void-like monistic mysticism often resists active seeking or training (Paper, 2004). Bharati (1961) referred to mysticism as a "zero-experience," noting that while it can temporarily disrupt one's ego perspective, it does not necessarily produce lasting or predictable changes in behavior or social interactions. Furthermore, most traditions expect those who undergo mystical experiences to return to the world and function within it, rather than dedicating their lives to the mere pursuit of mystical states.

Nor are there inherent logical connections between mysticism and morality (Wainwright, 1981). In some cases, mysticism may even undermine moral values, fostering an indifference to ethical considerations. Conversely, mysticism may reinforce morality by deepening attitudes that have ethical consequences. Christian mysticism, for example, integrates *caritas* (charity) as a central virtue, which Augustine regarded as an essential component of the beatific vision and contemplative life (Butler, 1922). Similarly, the Bodhisattva ideal in Mahayana Buddhism advocates postponing one's own liberation until all beings achieve enlightenment (Conze, 1959). However, monistic mysticism is not a necessary condition for the truth or falsity of any moral proposition. While nondualistic mysticism within theistic traditions may affirm the moral value of love and holiness, one does not need mystical consciousness to hold the conviction that love itself is morally significant.

Empirical studies remain relatively scarce in investigating the predictors and outcomes of mysticism, which, in large surveys, is often assessed with the item: "Did you ever have a religious or spiritual experience that changed your life?" Responses to the question are labeled as transformative religious or spiritual experiences (RSEs). A recent study employing an American representative sample of 10,529 young adults examined the associations between reporting a transformative RSE in late adolescence and a wide range of physical, mental, behavioral, and social health indicators assessed in early adulthood (Chen et al., 2025). Controlling for an extensive set of covariates, antecedents of transformative RSE included adverse childhood environments, negative parental dynamics, and heightened religious involvement. Consistent outcomes of transformative RSE involved both markers of vulnerability – such as post-traumatic stress disorder diagnosis and loneliness – and indicators of prosocial engagement, such as volunteering and voting. These findings point toward a double-edged sword effect of transformative RSE – both weakening the self and promoting connectedness with something greater.

6.4 Mundane Living

While this Element has explored various types and manifestations of mysticism, the crucial inquiry remains: where does mysticism lead? Once images, concepts, and the conscious ego dissolve, what remnants endure within the realm of intellectual life? If the realm of multiplicity dissipates, what form of unity emerges in its place? These are the questions that have been posed since the inception of empirical studies on mysticism (Maréchal, 2012). Our response is this: if there is a lesson to be learned from profound mystical states, it is how to return and live the mundane life as if it were divine (Aurobindo, 1990).

The greatest revelation is that everything lies in the here and now. Kornfield (2011) advocates for an "embodied enlightenment," integrating Western psychology with Buddhism and privileging the everyday householder's life as the site of awakening – an approach central to Humanistic Buddhism (*Renjian Fojiao*). Enlightenment is not found in the past or the future, nor in the depths of the cosmos. Cutsinger (1997) articulates the temporal dimension of spiritual awareness as follows: "There are two moments in life which are everything: the present moment, when we are free to choose what we would be, and the moment of death, when we have no longer any choice and the decision belongs to God" (p. 197). In a spatial sense, McKenna (1991) reminds us that "we have moved ourselves out toward the edge of the galaxy, when the fact is that the most richly organized material in the universe is the human cerebral cortex, and the densest and richest experience in the universe is the experience you are having right now" (p. 42).

This emphasis on lived experience is reflected in Gurdjieff's (1950) *Fourth Way*, which integrates spiritual practice into daily life rather than advocating monastic retreat, seeking to align the soul with universal principles. Mysticism underscores the transformative potential of harmonizing the three centers of human experience – thinking, feeling, and moving. Through the synthesis of contemplative exercises with practical tasks, this approach fosters both presence and inner growth. As envisioned by McKenna (1991), a possible future for humanity may involve an attempt to externalize the soul and internalize the body – first surpassing the confines of the physical form, then transcending cognition itself.

Many mystical traditions teach that the purpose of this reality is for the soul to learn and evolve. Among spiritist schools, there is a saying: the world is a school in which souls – sparks of divinity – are tutored and progress to higher levels, where suffering serves as a pedagogical tool and meaning is not simply inherited but realized (Hick, 2013). True scholarship unites *crede ut intelligas* ("believe in order to understand") and *intellige ut credas* ("understand in order to believe"), harmonizing intellect and will. Education, in this view, is not the mere accumulation of knowledge but the cultivation of understanding, for in traditional systems, to *know* is to *be*. There is no separation between the object and subject of knowledge (Quinn, 1997).

Ultimately, to *know* is to be freed from the illusion that there is something more to discover beyond what is already within. The unknown is not situated beyond the present boundaries of knowledge but at the very center of human being (Flood, 2013), here and now, as it has always been. It is not acquired but awakened to, as in Shankara's *Direct Experience of Reality*: "By the name of the world is denoted consciousness; negate the world and know it" (quoted in Nasr, 1981, p. 307). Thus, the Christian tradition affirms, "Ye shall know the truth, and the truth shall make you free" (John 8:32), while the Islamic prophet declares, "Say there is no divinity but the Divine and be delivered" (quoted in Nasr, 1981, p. 328).

All mystical learning ultimately leads to the recognition that one already possesses what one has been seeking. The mysticism is in the mundane. As Zhuangzi states in *What Comes from Without* (*Waiwu*), "The purpose of a fishnet is to catch fish; once the fish is caught, the net is forgotten. Words are employed to convey ideas; but when the ideas are apprehended, the words are forgotten."

6.5 Conclusion

By presenting a range of mystical experiences, this Element argues that between the extremes of highbrow monism and promiscuous relativism, there exists a path of committed pluralism – one that remains open to the vast diversity of human experience while being anchored in certain truth claims, albeit with an awareness of their limitations (James, 1909). As anthropologist Richard Shweder poetically observes (quoted in Kripal, 2008, p. 441), "The knowable world is incomplete if seen from any one point of view, incoherent if seen from all points of view at once, and empty if seen from nowhere in particular." The significance of mysticism extends beyond sacred knowledge, offering insights that inform and transform mundane existence. Indeed, its highest moral implication may be, in Einstein's words, to "live the life as though everything is a miracle." Or, as the fifteenth-century Indian poet Kabir puts it, it is not so much that the drop merges into the ocean as it is that the ocean is fully present in each drop.

Ultimately, mysticism transcends the confines of individual experience. In doing so, it expands our perception of ordinary reality and fundamentally transforms the one perceiving it. But what we define as "ordinary reality" is itself a social construction, shaped by physicalist, religious, spiritist, or other cultural frameworks. Beyond these constructs may lie an immeasurable spectrum of realities, and it is through the fractures of these realms that mysticism casts its light. It is possible that the universe is self-aware, awakening to itself through its conscious creations (Goswami, 1995). A Sufi hadith expresses this cosmological self-revelation: "I (the One) was a hidden treasure, and I desired to be known. So I brought forth creation in order that I might be known" (quoted in Awn, 2013, p. 253). The sigh of longing gives birth to the universe, the mirror in which the One comes to know itself.

If all that we can truly comprehend is experience, then, as McKenna (1991) insightfully notes, the densest and most profound experience in the universe must be found nowhere but in what we are living at this very moment. Consequently, the genuine human quest may not revolve around unraveling the meaning of life, but rather to attain "an experience of being alive, so that our life experiences on the purely physical plane will have resonances within our own innermost being and reality," in Joseph Campbell's words, "so that we actually feel the rapture of being alive" (*The Power of Myth*).

References

Abell, G. O. & Singer, B. (eds.) (1981). *Science and the paranormal: Probing the existence of the supernatural*. Scribners.

Albrecht, C. (2019). *Psychology of mystical consciousness* (F. K. Woehrer, Trans.). Crossroad. (Original work published 1951).

Almond, P. C. (1982). *Mystical experience and religious doctrine: An investigation of the study of mysticism in world religions*. Walter de Gruyter.

Anonymous. (2009). *Neizheng guancha biji: Zhentuben zhongyi jiepouxue gangmu*. [Notes from internal observation: Depicting the anatomy of Chinese medicine]. Guangxi Normal University.

Apffel-Marglin, F., & Gonzales, R. C. (2022). *Initiated by the spirits: Healing the ills of modernity through Shamanism, psychedelics and the power of the sacred*. Green Fire Press.

Atmanspacher, H., & Fuchs, C. A. (Eds.) (2014). *The Pauli-Jung conjecture and its impact today*. Imprint Academic.

Aurobindo, S. (1990). *The life divine*. Lotus Press. (Original work published 1909).

Awn, P. (2013). Sufism: An introduction. In S. T. Katz (ed.), *Comparative mysticism: An anthology of original sources* (pp. 247–255). Oxford University Press.

Bache, C. M. (2019). *LSD and the mind of the universe: Diamonds from heaven*. Park Street Press.

Barnard, G. W. (2022). *Liquid light: Ayahuasca spirituality and the Santo Daime tradition*. New York: Columbia University Press.

Barrett, F. S., Johnson, M. W., & Griffiths, R. R. (2015). Validation of the revised Mystical Experience Questionnaire in experimental sessions with psilocybin. *Journal of Psychopharmacology, 29*(11), 1182–1190.

Bastian, A. (1895). *Ethnische Elementargedanken in der Lehre vom Menschen*. Weidmann.

Bateson, G. (1979). *Mind and nature: A necessary unity*. E. P. Dutton.

Bellah, R. N. (2011). *Religion in human evolution*. Harvard University Press.

Belzen, J. A. (2009). *Towards cultural psychology of religion: Principles, approaches, applications*. Springer.

Bergson, H. (1988). *Matter and memory*. Zone Books. (Original work published 1896).

Bharati, A. (1961). *The ochre robe: An autobiography*. George Allen & Unwin.

Biernacki, L., & Clayton, P. (eds.). (2013). *Panentheism across the world's traditions*. Oxford University Press.
Bikkhu Bodhi. (ed.). (2005). *In the Buddha's words: An anthology of discourses from the Pali Canon*. Wisdom Publications.
Blackmore, S. J. (1982). *Beyond the body: An investigation of out-of-body experiences*. Paladin.
Blanke, O., Ortigue, S., Landis, T., & Seeck, M. (2002). Stimulating illusory own-body perceptions. *Nature, 419*(6904), 269–270.
Blavatsky, H. P. (1895). *The secret doctrine*. Theosophical Publishing Society.
Blofeld, J. (1970). *The tantric mysticism of Tibet*. E. P. Dutton.
Bohm, D. (1980). *Wholeness and the implicate order*. Routledge.
Bolton, R. (2014). Intuition in Aristotle. In L. M. Osbeck (ed.), *Rational intuition: Philosophical roots, scientific investigations* (pp. 39–54). Cambridge University Press.
Bucke, R. M. (1923). *Cosmic consciousness: A study in the evolution of the human mind*. E. P. Dutton.
Buhlman, W. (1996). *Adventures beyond the body: How to experience out-of-body travel*. HarperOne.
Butler, C. (1922). *Western mysticism: The teachings of SS Augustine, Gregory and Bernard on contemplation and the contemplative life*. E. P. Dutton.
Campbell, J. (1949). *The hero with a thousand faces*. Pantheon Books.
Campbell, J. (1959–1968). *The masks of God (Vols. 1–4)*. Viking Press.
Capra, F. (1975). *The Tao of physics: An exploration of the parallels between modern physics and eastern mysticism*. Shambhala.
Carhart-Harris, R. L., Erritzoe, D., Williams, T. et al. (2012). Neural correlates of the psychedelic state as determined by fMRI studies with psilocybin. *Proceedings of the National Academy of Sciences, 109*(6), 2138–2143.
Carhart-Harris, R. L., Friston, K. J., & Barker, E. L. (2019). REBUS and the anarchic brain: Toward a unified model of the brain action of psychedelics. *Pharmacological Reviews, 71*(3), 316–344.
Carhart-Harris, R. L., Muthukumaraswamy, S., Roseman, L. et al. (2016). Neural correlates of the LSD experience revealed by multimodal neuroimaging. *Proceedings of the National Academy of Sciences, 113*(17), 4853–4858.
Castaneda, C. (1968). *The teachings of Don Juan: A Yaqui way of knowledge*. University of California Press.
Castaneda, C. (1993). *The art of dreaming*. HarperCollins.
Chakrabarty, D. (2020). *Provincializing Europe: Postcolonial thought and historical difference*. Princeton University Press.

Chalmers, D. J. (1996). *The conscious mind: In search of a fundamental theory.* Oxford University Press.

Chen, Z. J. (2023, October). *Mystical experiences in Shamanic practices: A pluralistic view of the unity* [Paper presentation]. SSSR+RRA 2023 Annual Meeting, Salt Lake City, USA.

Chen, Z. J. (2025). Mysticism in Daoism: An overview and analysis. In D. Yaden & M. van Elk (eds.), *Oxford Handbook of Psychedelic, Religious, Spiritual, and Mystical Experiences.* Oxford University Press.

Chen, Z. J., Cowden, R., & Wilkinson, R. (2025). Between vulnerability and connection: Longitudinal evidence on the impact of transformative religious/spiritual experiences. *Stress and Health, 41*(5), e70110.

Chen, Z. J., & Ghorbani, N. (2024). Islamic mysticism and transliminality: Factor and network analysis in Iranian Muslim students. *Social Sciences & Humanities Open, 10,* e100979.

Chen, Z. J., Ghorbani, N., Watson, P. J., & Aghababaei, N. (2013). Muslim experiential religiousness and Muslim attitudes toward religion: Dissociation of experiential and attitudinal aspects of religiosity in Iran. *Studia Religiologica, 46*(1), 35–44.

Chen, Z. J., & Guo, S. (2025). Encompassing marvel of body and spirit: Daoist mysticism and interpretation. *Psychology of Religion and Spirituality, 17*(4), 447–459.

Chen, Z. J. & Guo, S. (in press). The psychology of religion in China – Eastern Tradition. In Ladd, K., Basu, J., DeMarinis, V., Ok, Ü., & Zangari, W. (eds.), *The Cambridge Handbook of the International Psychology of Religion.* Cambridge University Press.

Chen, Z. J., Guo, S., & Cowden, R. (2023). Enriching the common core of mystical experience: A qualitative analysis of interviews with Daoist monks and nuns. *International Journal of Psychology of Religion, 33*(4), 397–414.

Chen, Z. J. & Patel, J. (2021). Spiritual experiences in soulmate relationships: Qualitative and network analysis of the mystical bond. *International Journal for the Psychology of Religion, 31*(3), 176–188.

Chen, Z. J., Qi, W., Hood, R. W., Jr., & Watson, P. J. (2011a). Common Core Thesis and qualitative and quantitative study of Chinese Buddhist monks and nuns. *Journal for the Scientific Study of Religion, 50*(4), 654–670.

Chen, Z. J., Saucier, G., Hsu, G-Y., Zhou, X. (2018). Chinese isms dimensions in mainland China and Taiwan: Convergence and extension of American isms dimensions. *Journal of Personality, 86*(3), 555–571.

Chen, Z. J., Yang, L., Hood, R. W., Jr., & Watson, P. J. (2011b). Mystical experience in Tibetan Buddhists: Common core thesis revisited. *Journal for the Scientific Study of Religion, 50*(2), 328–338.

Chen, Z. J., Zhang, Y., Hood, R. W., Jr., & Watson, P. J. (2012). Mysticism in Chinese Christians and non-Christians: Measurement invariance of the Mysticism Scale and implications for the mean differences. *The International Journal for the Psychology of Religion, 22*(2), 155–168.

Clark, W. H. (1958). *The psychology of religion.* Macmillan.

Conze, E. (1959). *Buddhism: Its essence and development.* Harper & Brothers.

Coomaraswamy, A. (1943). *Hinduism and Buddhism.* Philosophical Library.

Coomaraswamy, A. K. (1977). *Selected papers, traditional art, and symbolism.* Princeton University Press.

Corbin, H. (1969). *Creative imagination in the Sufism of Ibn'Arabi.* Princeton University Press.

Corbin, H. (1977). *Spiritual body and celestial earth: From Mazdean Iran to Shi'ite Iran.* Princeton University Press.

Craffert, P. F., Baker, J. R., & Winkelman, M. J. (eds.). (2019). *The supernatural after the neuro-turn.* Routledge.

Crowley, M., & Shulgin, A. (2019). *Secret drugs of Buddhism: Psychedelic sacraments and the origins of the Vajrayana.* Synergetic Press.

Cutsinger, J. S. (1997). *Advice to the serious seeker: Meditations on the teaching of Frithjof Schuon.* SUNY Press.

Deikman, A. J. (1966). Deautomatization and the mystic experience. *Psychiatry: Journal for the Study of Interpersonal Processes, 29*(4), 324–338.

Doblin, R., & Burge, B. (eds.). (2014). *Manifesting minds: A review of psychedelics in science, medicine, sex, and spirituality.* North Atlantic Books.

Dodds, E. R. (1964). *The Greeks and the irrational.* University of California Press.

Dominguez, I. (2008). *Spirit Speak: Knowing and understanding spirit guides, ancestors, ghosts, angels, and the divine.* The Career Press.

Dudjom Rinpoche. (1991). *The Nyingma school of Tibetan Buddhism: Its fundamentals and history* (Gyurme Dorje, Trans.). Wisdom Publications.

Dumont, L. (1975). On the comparative understanding of non-modern civilizations. *Daedalus, 104*(2), 153–172.

Eckhart, M. (2009). The complete mystical works of Meister Eckhart (M. O'C. Walshe, Trans.). Crossroad.

Eliade, M. (1954). *The myth of the eternal return: Cosmos and history.* Princeton University Press.

Eliade, M. (1958). *Yoga: Immortality and freedom.* Princeton University Press.

Eliade, M. (1959). *The sacred and the profane: The nature of religion.* Harcourt.

Eliade, M. (1964). *Shamanism: Archaic techniques of ecstasy.* Princeton University Press.

Eliade, M. (1978–1985). *A history of religious ideas (Vol 1–3)*. University of Chicago Press.

Elkin, A. P. (1977). *Aboriginal men of high degree: Initiation and sorcery in the world's oldest tradition*. University of Queensland Press.

Ernst, C. W. (1997). *Sufism: An introduction to the mystical tradition of Islam*. Shambhala.

Faivre, A. (1994). *Access to Western esotericism*. SUNY Press.

Faivre, A. (2000). *Theosophy, imagination, tradition: Studies in Western esotericism* (C. Rhone, Trans.). SUNY Press.

Faivre, A., & Needleman, J. (eds.). (1992). *Modern esoteric spirituality*. Crossroad.

Fakhry, M. (2004). *A history of Islamic philosophy*. Columbia University Press.

Ferrer, J. N., & Sherman, J. H. (eds.). (2008). *The participatory turn: Spirituality, mysticism, religious studies*. SUNY Press.

Flattery, D. S., & Schwartz, M. (1989). *Haoma and harmaline: the botanical identity of the Indo-Iranian sacred hallucinogen" soma" and its legacy in religion, language, and Middle-Eastern folklore*. University of California Press.

Flood, G. (2013). *The truth within: A history of inwardness in Christianity, Hinduism and Buddhism*. Oxford University Press.

Forman, R. K. C. (ed.) (1990). *The problem of pure consciousness*. Oxford University Press.

Forman, R. K. C. (1999). *Mysticism, mind, consciousness*. SUNY Press.

Fort, C. (1932). *Wild talents: A collection of rare phenomena*. Kendall.

Gallagher, C., Kumar, V. K., & Pekala, R. J. (1994). The anomalous experiences inventory: Reliability and validity. *Journal of Parapsychology*, 58(4), 402–428.

Gallimore, A. R. (2019). *Alien information theory: Psychedelic drug technologies and the cosmic game*. Strange Worlds Press.

Goleman, D., & Davidson, R. J. (2018). *Altered traits: Science reveals how meditation changes your mind, brain, and body*. Penguin.

Gossen, G. H., & León-Portilla, M. (eds.). (1993). *South and Meso-American native spirituality: From the cult of the feathered serpent to the theology of liberation*. Crossroad.

Goswami, A. (1995). *The self-aware universe*. J. P. Tarcher.

Govinda, L. A. (1969). *Foundations of Tibetan mysticism*. Weiser Books.

Green, A. (ed.). (1987). *Jewish Spirituality* (2 vols). Crossroad.

Greer, J. C. (2025). Historians on drugs: Toward an empirical historiography of global psychedelic cultures. *South Atlantic Quarterly*, 124(2), 263–293.

Griffiths, R. R., Johnson, M. W., Richards, W. A. et al. (2011). Psilocybin occasioned mystical-type experiences: Immediate and persisting dose-related effects. *Psychopharmacology, 218*, 649–665.

Griffiths, R. R., Richards, W. A., McCann, U., & Jesse, R. (2006). Psilocybin can occasion mystical-type experiences having substantial and sustained personal meaning and spiritual significance. *Psychopharmacology, 187*, 268–283.

Grim, J. (2013). Native American mystical traditions: An introduction. In S. T. Katz (ed.), *Comparative mysticism: An anthology of original sources* (pp. 539–552). Oxford University Press.

Greeley, A. M. (1975). *The sociology of the paranormal: A reconnaissance.* Sage.

Grof, S. (1998). *The cosmic game: Explorations of the frontiers of human consciousness.* SUNY Press.

Grof, S. (2019). *The way of the psychonaut: Encyclopedia for inner journeys* (2 Vols.). MAPS.

Guénon, R. (1945). *Introduction to the study of the Hindu doctrines.* Luzac.

Guénon, R. (2009). Islamic esotericism. In J. Herlihy (ed.), *The essential René Guénon: Metaphysics, tradition, and the crisis of modernity* (pp. 206–211). World Wisdom.

Gurdjieff, G. I. (1950). *Beelzebub's tales to his grandson: An objectively impartial criticism of the life of man.* Harcourt, Brace.

Gyatso, J. (1998). *Apparitions of the self: The secret autobiographies of a Tibetan visionary.* Princeton University Press.

Hakl, H. T. (2014). *Eranos: An alternative intellectual history of the twentieth century.* Routledge.

Hall, M. P. (2007). *The secret teachings of all ages.* Wilder Publications.

Hancock, G. (2006). *Supernatural: Meetings with the ancient teachers of mankind.* Red Wheel Weiser.

Hanegraaff, W. J. (2022). *Hermetic spirituality and the historical imagination: Altered states of knowledge in late antiquity.* Cambridge University Press.

Harner, M. (1980). *The way of the Shaman: A guide to power and healing.* HarperOne.

Harner, M. (2013). *Cave and cosmos: Shamanic encounters with another reality.* North Atlantic Books.

Henry, J. (ed.). (2004). *Parapsychology: Research on exceptional experiences.* Routledge.

Hick, J. (2013). *The fifth dimension: An exploration of the spiritual realm.* Simon and Schuster.

Hilton, W. (1990). *The scale of perfection* (J. P. H. Clark & R. Dorward, Trans.). Paulist Press.

Holbraad, M., & Pedersen, M. A. (2017). *The ontological turn: An anthropological exposition.* Cambridge University Press.

Hollenback, J. (1996). *Mysticism: Experience, response, and empowerment.* Penn State Press.

Hood, R. W., Jr. (1975). The construction and preliminary validation of a measure of reported mystical experience. *Journal for the Scientific Study of Religion, 14*(1), 29–41.

Hood, R. W., Jr. (1977). Eliciting mystical states of consciousness with semi-structured nature experiences. *Journal for the Scientific Study of Religion, 16*(2), 155–163.

Hood, R. W., Jr. (2006). The common core thesis in the study of mysticism. In P. McNamara (ed.), *Where God and science meet, Vol. 3* (pp. 119–138). Praeger.

Hood, R. W., Jr., & Chen, Z. J. (2012). Social scientific study of Christian mysticism. In J. Lamm (ed.), *Blackwell companion to Christian mysticism* (pp. 577–591). John Wiley & Sons.

Hood, R. W., Jr. & Chen, Z. J. (2013). Mystical, spiritual, and religious experiences. In R. Paloutzian & C. Park (eds.), *Handbook of the psychology of religion and spirituality*, 2nd ed. (pp. 422–440). Guilford.

Hood, R. W., Jr., Hill, P. C., & Spilka, B. (2018). *The psychology of religion: An empirical approach.* Guilford Press.

Hood, R. W., Jr. & Morris, R. J. (1981). Sensory isolation and the differential elicitation of religious imagery in intrinsic and extrinsic persons. *Journal for the Scientific Study of Religion, 20*(3), 261–273.

Houran, J., Thalbourne, M. A., & Lange, R. (2003). Methodological note: Erratum and comment on the use of the revised transliminality scale. *Consciousness and Cognition, 12*(1), 140–144.

Hovmand, O. R., Poulsen, E. D., & Arnfred, S. (2024). Assessment of the acute subjective psychedelic experience: A review of patient-reported outcome measures in clinical research on classical psychedelics. *Journal of Psychopharmacology, 38*(1), 19–32.

Hultkrantz, Å. (1979). *The religions of the American Indians* (M. Setterwall, Trans.). University of California Press.

Hultkrantz, Å. (1987). *Native religions of North America: The power of visions and fertility.* Harper & Row.

Huss, B. (2020). *Mystifying Kabbalah: Academic scholarship, national theology, and new age spirituality.* Oxford University Press.

Huxley, A. (1945). *The perennial philosophy.* Harper & Brothers.

References

Huxley, A. (1954). *The doors of perception and heaven and hell*. Harper & Brothers.

Idel, M. (1988). *Kabbalah: New perspectives*. Yale University Press.

Idel, M. (1995). *Hasidism: Between ecstasy and magic*. SUNY Press.

Idel, M. (2013). Jewish mysticism: An introduction. In S. T. Katz (ed.), *Comparative mysticism: An anthology of original sources* (pp. 25–36). Oxford University Press.

James, W. (1899). *Human immortality: Two supposed objections to the doctrine*. Archibald Constable.

James, W. (1902). *The varieties of religious experience. A study in human nature*. Longmans, Green.

James, W. (1909). *A pluralistic universe: Hibbert Lectures at Manchester College on the present situation in philosophy*. Longmans, Green.

Jaynes, J. (1976). *The origin of consciousness in the breakdown of the bicameral mind*. Houghton Mifflin.

Johnson, D. (1994). *Body, spirit and democracy*. North Atlantic Books.

Johnson, M. W., Hendricks, P. S., Barrett, F. S., & Griffiths, R. R. (2019). Classic psychedelics: An integrative review of epidemiology, therapeutics, mystical experience, and brain network function. *Pharmacology & Therapeutics*, *197*, 83–102.

Jones, R. H. (1986). *Science and mysticism: A comparative study of Western natural science, Theravada Buddhism, and Advaita Vedanta*. Associated University Presses.

Jones, R. H. (2016). *Philosophy of mysticism: Raids on the ineffable*. SUNY Press.

Jones, R. & Gellman, J. (2022, Fall). Mysticism. In E. N. Zalta & U. Nodelman (eds.), *The Stanford Encyclopedia of Philosophy*. plato.stanford.edu/archives/fall2022/entries/mysticism/.

Jordan, D. K., & Overmyer, D. L. (1986). *The flying phoenix: Aspects of Chinese sectarianism in Taiwan*. Princeton University Press.

Jung, C. G. (1953). *Psychology and religion: West and east*. Princeton University Press.

Kardec, A. (1857). *The Spirits' Book*. Luchnos.

Katz, S. T. (ed.). (1978). *Mysticism and philosophical analysis*. Oxford University Press.

Katz, S. T. (ed.). (1983). *Mysticism and religious traditions*. Oxford University Press.

Katz, S. T. (ed.). (1992). *Mysticism and language*. Oxford University Press.

Katz, S. T. (ed.). (2000). *Mysticism and sacred scripture*. Oxford University Press.

Katz, S. T. (ed.). (2013). *Comparative mysticism: An anthology of original sources*. Oxford University Press.

Kelly, E. F., Kelly, E. W., Crabtree, A., Gauld, A., & Grosso, M. (eds.) (2007). *Irreducible mind: Toward a psychology for the 21st century*. Rowman & Littlefield.

Kelly, E. F., Crabtree, A., & Marshall, P. (eds.). (2015). *Beyond physicalism: Toward reconciliation of science and spirituality*. Rowman & Littlefield.

Kelly, E. F., & Marshall, P. (eds.). (2021). *Consciousness unbound: Liberating mind from the tyranny of materialism*. Rowman & Littlefield.

Kohn, L. (1993). *The Taoist experience: An anthology*. SUNY Press.

Kohn, L. (2013). Confucianism and Daoism: An introduction. In S. T. Katz (ed.), *Comparative mysticism: An anthology of original sources* (pp. 479–486). Oxford University Press.

Kongtrul, J. (2007). *The treasury of knowledge: Book eight, part four: Esoteric instructions: A detailed presentation of the process of meditation in Vajrayāna* (S. Harding, Trans.). Snow Lion.

Kornfield, J. (2011). *Bringing home the Dharma: Awakening right where you are*. Shambhala Publications.

Kripal, J. J. (2008). *Esalen: America and the religion of no religion*. University of Chicago Press.

Kripal, J. J. (2010). *Authors of the impossible: The paranormal and the sacred*. University of Chicago Press.

Krishna, G. (1971). *Kundalini: The evolutionary energy in man*. Shambhala.

Kunzang Lama. (1993). *Kun-zang la-may zhal-lung: The oral instruction of Kun-zang La-ma on the preliminary practices of Dzog-Chen Long-Chen Nying-Tig*. Diamond-Lotus.

La Barre, W. (1972). *The ghost dance: Origins of religion*. Allen & Unwin.

Laszlo, E. (2004). *Science and the Akashic Field: An integral theory of everything*. Inner Traditions.

Latour, B. (1988). *The pasteurization of France*. Harvard University Press.

Latour, B. (1993). *We have never been modern*. Harvard University Press.

Latour, B. (2013). *An inquiry into modes of existence: An anthropology of the moderns*. Harvard University Press.

Leary, T. (1998). *The politics of ecstasy*. Ronin.

Lewis, F. D. (2000). *Rumi: Past and present, East and West: The life, teachings, and poetry of Jalâl al-Din Rumi*. Oneworld Publications.

Li, S.-C. (2018). *Lingjie de kexue* [The science of the spiritual world]. San Cai Culture.

Lindahl, J. R., Fisher, N. E., Cooper, D. J., Rosen, R. K., & Britton, W. B. (2017). The varieties of contemplative experience: A mixed-methods study of meditation-related challenges in Western Buddhists. *PloS one, 12*(5), e0176239.

Luckmann, T. (1967). *The invisible religion.* Macmillan.

Ludwig, A. M. (1966). Altered states of consciousness. *Archives of General Psychiatry, 15*(3), 225–234.

Luhrmann, T. M. (2020). *How God becomes real: Kindling the presence of invisible others.* Princeton University Press.

Luhrmann, T. M., Weisman, K., Aulino, F. et al. (2021). Sensing the presence of gods and spirits across cultures and faiths. *Proceedings of the National Academy of Sciences, 118*(5), e2016649118.

MacLean, P. D. (1990). *The triune brain in evolution.* Plenum Press.

Maréchal, J. (2012). *The psychology of the mystics* (A. Thorold, Trans.). Dover. (Original work published 1927).

Marshall, P. (2019). *The shape of the soul: What mystical experience tells us about ourselves and reality.* Roman & Littlefield.

Maupin, E. W. (1972). On meditation. In A. Tart (ed.), *Altered states of consciousness* (pp. 181–190). Anchor Books.

McGilchrist, I. (2019). *The master and his emissary: The divided brain and the making of the western world.* Yale University Press.

McGinn, B. (1991). *The foundations of mysticism: Origins to the fifth century.* Crossroad.

McGinn, B. (1998). *The flowering of mysticism.* Crossroad.

McGinn, B. (2006). *The essential writings of Christian mysticism.* Modern Library.

McGinn, B. (2013). Christian mysticism: An introduction. In S. T. Katz (ed.), *Comparative mysticism: An anthology of original sources* (pp. 157–162). Oxford University Press.

McGinn, B. (2021). *The crisis of mysticism: Quietism in seventeenth-century Spain, Italy, and France.* Crossroad.

McKenna, T. (1991). *The archaic revival.* HarperSanFrancisco.

McKenna, T. (1992). *Food of the Gods: The search for the original tree of knowledge.* Bantam.

Merkur, D. (1998). *The ecstatic imagination: Psychedelic experiences and the psychoanalysis of self-actualization.* SUNY Press.

Merkur, D. (2010). *Explorations of the psychoanalytic mystics.* Rodolphi.

Merleau-Ponty, M. (1962). *Phenomenology of perception.* Routledge.

Mensky, M. B. (2010). *Consciousness and quantum mechanics: Life in parallel worlds-miracles of consciousness from quantum reality.* World Scientific.

Metzner, R. (ed.) (2006). *Sacred vine of spirits: Ayahuasca.* Park Street Press.

Metzner, R. (2022). *The unfolding self: Varieties of transformative experience*. Synergetic Press.

Michaelson, J. (2011). *God in your body: Kabbalah, mindfulness and embodied spiritual practice*. Turner Publishing.

Moody, R. A. (1975). *Life after life: The investigation of a phenomenon – Survival of bodily death*. Bantam Books.

Mosurinjohn, S., & Ascough, R. (2025). Psychedelics, Eleusis, and the Invention of Religious Experience. *Psychedelic Medicine*. https://doi.org/10.1177/28314425251361835

Muraresku, B. C. (2020). *The immortality key: The secret history of the religion with no name*. St. Martin's Press.

Murphy, M. (1992). *The future of the body: Explorations into the further evolution of human nature*. Penguin Putnam.

Myers, F. W. H. (1903). *Human personality and its survival of bodily death* (2 vols). Longmans, Green.

Naranjo, C. (1976). Meditation: Its spirit and techniques. In C. Naranjo & Ornstein, R. E., *On the psychology of meditation* (pp. 3–132). Penguin Books.

Naranjo, C. (2006). *The way of silence and the talking cure: On meditation and psychotherapy*. Blue Dolphin.

Narby, J. (1999). *The cosmic serpent: DNA and the origins of knowledge*. Putnam.

Nasr, S. H. (1981). *Knowledge and the sacred*. Crossroad.

Nasr, S. H. (ed.) (1991). *Islamic spirituality* (2 vols). Crossroad.

Nasr, S. H. (2007). *The garden of truth: The vision and promise of Sufism, Islam's mystical tradition*. HarperCollins.

Neumann, E. (1954). *The origins and history of consciousness* (R. F. C. Hull, Trans.). Princeton University Press.

Newberg, A. (2018). *Neurotheology: How science can enlighten us about spirituality*. Columbia University Press.

Newberg, A. (2024). *Sex, God, and the brain: How sexual pleasure gave birth to religion and a whole lot more*. Turner.

Nietzsche, F. (1909). *Beyond good and evil: Prelude to a philosophy of the future*. T. N. Foulis.

Nikhilananda, S. (1942). *The Gospel of Sri Ramakrishna*. Ramakrishna-Vivekananda Center.

Norbu, N. (2013). *The light of Kailash: A history of Zhang Zhung and Tibet* (3 vols). North Atlantic Books.

Obeyesekere, G. (2012). *The awakened ones: Phenomenology of visionary experience*. Columbia University Press.

Olupona, J. K. (2000). *African spirituality: Forms, meanings and expressions*. Crossroad.

Otto, R. (1917). *Das Heilige*. Verlag von Wilhelm Engelmann.

Otto, R. (1932). *Mysticism east and west: A comparative analysis of the nature of mysticism*. Macmillan.

Owens, J., Cook, E. W., & Stevenson, I. (1990). Features of "near-death experience" in relation to whether or not patients were near death. *The Lancet, 336*(8724), 1175–1177.

Pahnke, W. N. (1969). Psychedelic drugs and mystical experience. *International Psychiatry Clinics, 5*(4), 149–162.

Pahnke, W. N., & Richards, W. A. (1966). Implications of LSD and experimental mysticism. *Journal of Religion and Health, 5*(3), 175–208.

Panksepp, J. & Biven, L. (2012). *The archaeology of mind: Neuroevolutionary origins of human emotion*. W. W. Norton.

Paper, J. (2004). *The mystic experience: A descriptive and comparative analysis*. SUNY Press.

Parsons, W. B. (2018). Mysticism in translation: Psychological advances, cautionary tales. In T. Cattoi & D. M. Odorisio (eds.), *Depth psychology and mysticism* (pp. 127–149). Palgrave Macmillan.

Partridge, C. H. (2018). *High culture: Drugs, mysticism, and the pursuit of transcendence in the modern world*. Oxford University Press.

Perry, W. N. (1981). *A treasury of traditional wisdom*. Perennial Books.

Pinchbeck, D. (2002). *Breaking open the head: A psychedelic journey into the heart of contemporary shamanism*. Broadway Books.

Plotinus. (1956). *The Enneads*. (S. MacKenna, Trans.). Faber and Faber.

Pregadio, F. (ed.). (2009). *Awakening to reality: The" Regulated Verses" of the Wuzhen pian, a Taoist classic of internal alchemy*. Golden Elixir Press.

Previc, F. (2009). *The Dopaminergic mind in human evolution and history*. Cambridge University Press.

Pribram, K. (1971). *Languages of the brain*. Prentice Hall.

Proudfoot, W. (1985). *Religious experience*. University of California Press.

Quinn, W. W. (1997). *The only tradition*. SUNY Press.

Radin, D. I. (1997). *The conscious universe: The scientific truth of psychic phenomena*. Harper Edge.

Radin, D. (2013). *Supernormal: Science, yoga, and the evidence for extraordinary psychic abilities*. Deepak Chopra Books.

Radin, D. (2018). *Real magic: Ancient wisdom, modern science, and a guide to the secret power of the universe*. Harmony Books.

Reichel-Dolmatoff, G. (1978). *Beyond the Milky Way: Hallucinatory imagery of the Tukano Indians*. UCLA Latin America Center Publications.

Reichenbach, K. B. von. (1850). *Researches on magnetism, electricity, heat, light, crystallization, and chemical attraction in their relations to the vital force* (W. Gregory, Trans.). Taylor, Walton and Maberly.

Richards, W. (2015). *Sacred knowledge*. Columbia University Press.

Roth, H. (2021). *The contemplative foundations of classical Daoism*. SUNY Press.

Ruck, C. A. (2018). *The son conceived in Drunkenness: Magical plants in the world of the Greek hero*. Regent Press & Entheomedia.

Said, E. W. (1978). *Orientalism*. Pantheon Books.

Sarter, M., Berntson, G. G., & Cacioppo, J. T. (1996). Brain imaging and cognitive neuroscience: Toward strong inference in attributing function to structure. *American psychologist*, *51*(1), 13–21.

Scheid, V. (2007). *Currents of tradition in Chinese medicine*: 1626–2006. Eastland Press.

Schimmel, A. (1994). *Deciphering the signs of God: A phenomenological approach to Islam*. University of North Carolina Press.

Scholem, G. (1961). *Major trends in Jewish mysticism*. Schocken.

Scholem, G. (1987). *Origins of the Kabbalah*. Princeton University Press.

Schultes, R. E., Hofmann, R., & Rätsch, C. (1992). *The plants of the Gods: Their sacred, healing, and hallucinogenic powers*. Healing Arts Press.

Schuon, F. (1953). *The transcendent unity of religions*. Faber & Faber.

Semkiw, W. (2011). *Origin of the soul and the purpose of reincarnation*. Pluto Project.

Shankara. (1947). *Crest-jewel of discrimination (Viveka Chudamani)* (S. Prabhavananda & C. Isherwood, Trans.). Vedanta Society.

Shanon, B. (2002). *The antipodes of the mind: Charting the phenomenology of the ayahuasca experience*. Oxford University Press.

Shanon, B. (2008). Biblical entheogens: A speculative hypothesis. *Time and Mind*, *1*(1), 51–74.

Sharf, R. H. (1998). Experience. In M. Taylor (ed.), *Critical terms for religious studies* (pp. 94–116). The University of Chicago Press.

Sharma, A. (2013). Hinduism: An introduction. In S. T. Katz (ed.), *Comparative mysticism: An anthology of original sources* (pp. 323–327). Oxford University Press.

Sheldrake, R. (1981). *A new science of life*. Tarcher.

Shulgin, A., & Shulgin, A. (1991). *PIHKAL: A chemical love story*. Transform Press.

Shulgin, A., & Shulgin, A. (1997). *TIHKAL: The continuation*. Transform Press.

Siegel, J. S., Subramanian, S., Perry, D. et al. (2024). Psilocybin desynchronizes the human brain. *Nature, 632*(8023), 131–138.

Sivaraman, K. (Ed.). (1989). *Hindu spirituality: Vedas through Vedanta*. Crossroad.

Smart, N. (1965). Interpretation and mystical experience. *Religious Studies 1*, 75–87.

Smith, H. (1976). *Forgotten truth: The common vision of the world's religions*. HarperCollins.

Smith, H. (2000). *Cleansing the doors of perception: The religious significance of entheogenic plants and chemicals*. Sentient Publications.

Spiegelberg, F. (1948). *The religion of no-religion*. James Ladd Delkin.

Staal, F. (1975). *Exploring mysticism: A methodological essay*. University of California Press.

Stace, W. (1960). *Mysticism and philosophy*. J. B. Lippincott.

Stapp, H. P. (2007). *Mindful universe: Quantum mechanics and the participating observer*. Springer.

Steiner, R. (1913). *An outline of esoteric science*. Anthroposophic Press.

Stevenson, I. (1974). *Twenty cases suggestive of reincarnation*. University of Virginia Press.

Stevenson, I. (2001). *Children who remember previous lives: A question of reincarnation*. McFarland.

Stewart, K. (1972). Dream theory in Malaya. In A. Tart (ed.), *Altered states of consciousness* (pp. 161–170). Anchor Books.

Strassman, R. (2000). *DMT: The spirit molecule*. Park Street Press.

Strassman, R. (2014). *DMT and the soul of prophecy: A new science of spiritual revelation in the Hebrew Bible*. Park Street Press.

Streib, H. & Chen, Z. J. (2021). Evidence for the brief Mysticism Scale: Psychometric properties, moderation and mediation effects in predicting spiritual self-identification. *International Journal for the Psychology of Religion, 31*(3), 165–175.

Studstill, R. (2005). *The unity of mystical traditions: The transformation of consciousness in Tibetan and German mysticism*. Brill.

Suzuki, D. T. (1959). *Zen and Japanese culture*. Princeton University Press.

Tafur, J. (2017). *The fellowship of the river: A medical doctor's exploration into traditional Amazonian plant medicine*. Espiritu Books.

Takeuchi, Y. (ed.). (1993). *Buddhist spirituality: Indian, Southeast Asian, Tibetan, early Chinese*. Crossroad.

Takeuchi, Y. (ed.). (1999). *Buddhist spirituality: Later China, Korea, Japan, and the modern world*. Crossroad.

Tart, C. T. (1972). *Altered states of consciousness*. Anchor Books.

Taves, A., & Barlev, M. (2023). A feature-based approach to the comparative study of "nonordinary" experiences. *American Psychologist, 78*(1), 50–61.

Taves, A., Ihm, E., Wolf, M. et al. (2023). The inventory of nonordinary experiences (INOE): Evidence of validity in the United States and India. *PloS one, 18*(7), e0287780.

Taylor, C. (2007). *The secular age*. Harvard University Press.

Taylor, J. G. (1980). *Science and the supernatural: An investigation of paranormal phenomena including psychic healing, clairvoyance, telepathy, and precognition*. E. P. Dutton.

Tellegen, A., & Atkinson, G. (1974). Openness to absorbing and self-altering experiences ("absorption"), a trait related to hypnotic susceptibility. *Journal of Abnormal Psychology, 83*(3), 268–277.

Teresa of Ávila. (1979). *The interior castle* (K. Kavanaugh & O. Rodriguez, Trans.). Paulist Press.

Thalbourne, M. A., & Delin, P. S. (1994). A common thread underlying belief in the paranormal, creative personality, mystical experience and psychopathology. *Journal of Parapsychology, 58*(1), 3–38.

Troeltsch, E. (1931). *The social teaching of the Christian churches*. Allen & Unwin.

Trungpa, C. (2013). *The tantric path of indestructible wakefulness: The profound treasury of the ocean of dharma*. Shambhala.

Tu, W., & Tucker, M. E. (eds.). (2003). *Confucian spirituality* (2 vols). Crossroad.

Tucker, J. B. (2005). *Life before life: A scientific investigation of children's memories of previous lives*. St. Martin's Press.

Tumminia, D. (2007). *Alien worlds: Social and religious dimensions of extraterrestrial contact*. University of California Press.

Underhill, E. (1911). *Mysticism: A study in the nature and development of man's spiritual consciousness*. Routledge.

Underwood, L. G. (2011). The daily spiritual experience scale: Overview and results. *Religions, 2*(1), 29–50.

Vallée, J. (1991). *The invisible college: What a group of scientists has discovered about UFO influences on the human mind*. Houghton Mifflin.

Van der Braak, A. (2023). *Ayahuasca as liquid divinity: An ontological approach*. Rowman & Littlefield.

Van Eeden, F. (1913). A study of dreams. *Proceedings of the Society for Psychical Research, 26*, 431–461.

Vargas, M. V., Dunlap, L. E., Dong, C. et al. (2023). Psychedelics promote neuroplasticity through the activation of intracellular 5-HT2A receptors. *Science, 379*(6633), 700–706.

Viveiros de Castro, E. (2014). *Cannibal metaphysics: For a post-structural anthropology* (P. Skafish, Trans.). University of Minnesota Press.

Wittmann, M. (2018). *Altered states of consciousness: Experiences out of time and self.* MIT Press.

Vivekananda, S. (2016). *Raja yoga or conquering the internal nature.* Advaita Ashrama. (Original published 1896).

Wahbeh, H., Yount, G., Vieten, C., Radin, D., & Delorme, A. (2020). Measuring extraordinary experiences and beliefs: a validation and reliability study. *F1000Research, 8,* 1741.

Wainwright (1981). *Mysticism: A study of its nature, cognitive value, and moral implications.* University of Wisconsin Press.

Wallace, B. A. (2015). *Dudjom Lingpa's visions of the Great Perfection.* Wisdom Publications.

Wasson, R. G. (1971). *Soma: Divine mushroom of immortality.* Harcourt, Brace, & World.

Wasson, R. G., Hofmann, A., & Ruck, C. A. (1978). *The road to Eleusis: Unveiling the secret of the mysteries.* Harcourt Brace Jovanovich.

Watson, C. W., & Ellen, R. (eds.). (1993). *Understanding witchcraft and sorcery in Southeast Asia.* University of Hawaii Press.

Watts, A. (1961). *Psychotherapy east & west.* Pantheon Books.

Weiner, H. (1969). *9 1/2 mystics: The Kabbala today.* Collier Books.

White, R. A. (1997). Exceptional human experiences and the experiential paradigm. In C. T. Tart (ed.), *Body mind spirit: Exploring the parapsychology of spirituality* (pp. 83–100). Hampton Road.

Wilber, K. (2017). *The religion of tomorrow: A vision for the future of the great traditions-more inclusive, more comprehensive, more complete.* Shambhala.

Wildman, W. (2010). *Religious philosophy as multidisciplinary comparative inquiry: Envisioning a future for the philosophy of religion.* SUNY Press.

Williamson, W. P., Hood, R. W., & Chen, Z. J. (2019). The god mysticism scale: A brief version. *Journal of Pastoral Psychology, 68*(3), 345–356.

Winkelman, M. (2010). *Shamanism: A biopsychosocial paradigm of consciousness and healing* (2nd ed.). ABC-CLIO.

Wittgenstein, L. (1953). *Philosophical investigations.* Blackwell.

Woods, J. H. (1914). *The Yoga-system of Patañjali.* Harvard University Press.

Xiong, S. (1932). *New treatise on the uniqueness of consciousness* (Xin weishi lun). (J. Makeham, Trans.). Yale University Press.

Xiong, S. (1945). *Dujing shiyao* [Essentials of Reading the Classics]. China Renmin University Press.

Yaden, D. B., & Newberg, A. (2022). *The varieties of spiritual experience: 21st century research and perspectives.* Oxford University Press.

Zaehner, R. C. (1957). *Mysticism sacred and profane: An inquiry into some varieties of preternatural experience*. Oxford University Press.

Zaleski, C. (1987). *Otherworld journeys: Accounts of near-death experience in medieval and modern times*. Oxford University Press.

Zimmer, H. R. (1946). *Myths and symbols in Indian art and civilization*. Princeton University Press.

Zimmer, H. R. (1951). *Philosophies of India*. Princeton University Press.

Zhang, S. H. (2009). *Jingzhuan zhuzi Yuxuan*. [Selections from the classics and commentaries]. China Renmin University Press.

Acknowledgment

This project is partially supported by a grant from Templeton World Charity Foundation (#32539), doi.org/10.54224/32539

Dedicated to Ralph W. Hood, Jr. and my late parents.

Psychology of Religion

Jonathan Lewis-Jong
St Mary's University Twickenham and University of Oxford

Jonathan Lewis-Jong is Researcher in Psychology of Religion at the Benedict XVI Centre for Religion and Society at St Mary's University, Twickenham, and an Associate of the Ian Ramsey Centre for Science and Religion at the University of Oxford. His recent books include *Experimenting with Religion* (2023) and *Death Anxiety and Religion Belief* (2016). He is also an Associate Editor at the American Psychological Association journal *Psychology of Religion and Spirituality*.

Editorial Board

Paul Bloom, *University of Toronto*
Adam B. Cohen, *Arizona State University*
Ara Norenzayan, *University of British Columbia*
Crystal Park, *University of Connecticut*
Aiyana Willard, *Brunel University*
Jacqueline Woolley, *University of Texas at Austin*

About the Series

This series offers authoritative introductions to central topics in the psychology of religion, covering the psychological causes, consequences, and correlates of religion, as well as conceptual and methodological issues. The Elements reflect diverse perspectives, including from developmental, evolutionary, cognitive, social, personality and clinical psychology, and neuroscience.

Cambridge Elements $^{\equiv}$

Psychology of Religion

Elements in the Series

Divination: A Cognitive Perspective
Ze Hong

Morality and the Gods
Benjamin Grant Purzycki

The Psychology of Mysticism
Zhuo Job Chen

A full series listing is available at: www.cambridge.org/EPOR

For EU product safety concerns, contact us at Calle de José Abascal, 56–1°,
28003 Madrid, Spain or eugpsr@cambridge.org.

www.ingramcontent.com/pod-product-compliance
Ingram Content Group UK Ltd.
Pitfield, Milton Keynes, MK11 3LW, UK
UKHW022047110326
468905UK00021B/2471